hachette
BOOKS

LARGE
PRINT

BLOWING

THE BLOODY

DOORS OFF

AND OTHER

LESSONS IN LIFE

MICHAEL CAINE

hachette
BOOKS

LARGE PRINT EDITION

Hachette Books
Hachette Book Group
1290 Avenue of the Americas, New York, NY 10104
hachettebooks.com
twitter.com/hachettebooks

Originally published in Great Britain in 2018 by Hodder & Stoughton

A Hachette UK company

First U.S. Edition: October 2018

Hachette Books is a division of Hachette Book Group, Inc. The Hachette Books name and logo are trademarks of Hachette Book Group, Inc.

The publisher is not responsible for websites (or their content) that are not owned by the publisher.

Library of Congress Control Number: 2018953662

ISBNs: 978-0-316-45119-2 (hardcover), 978-0-316-45187-1 (large print), 978-0-316-45116-1 (ebook)

Printed in the United States of America

LSC-C

10 9 8 7 6 5 4 3 2 1

For Shakira, Niki, Natasha, Taylor,
Allegra and Miles—and for you.

Contents

Introduction

THE FIRST TIME I was in the United States, when I had just made *Alfie*, I was sitting on my own in the lobby of the Beverly Hills Hotel and heard the sound of a helicopter landing in the gardens opposite. This, the porter told me, was strictly illegal. He and I stood at the door to see who was so flagrantly flouting the law—presumably the President, of the United States or at least of the Beverly Hills Hotel. Across Sunset Boulevard, out of a swirling sun-flecked cloud of dust, six foot four and in full cowboy get-up, strode the unmistakable figure of John Wayne. As I stood there with my mouth open he caught my eye and altered his course to come over to me. "What's your name, kid?" he asked.

"Michael Caine," I managed to croak.

"That's right," he agreed, with a tilt of his head. "You were in that movie *Alfie*."

"Yes," I said. I wasn't really keeping up my end of the conversation.

"You're gonna be a star, kid," he drawled, draping his arm around my shoulders. "But if you want to stay one, remember this: talk low, talk slow, and don't say too much."

"Thank you, Mr. Wayne," I said.

"Call me Duke." He gave me a chuck on the arm, turned around and swaggered off.

It was a mind-blowing Hollywood moment for an ambitious young actor on his first visit to the city of dreams. And it was great advice for anyone who was going to be acting in Westerns and delivering all his dialogue from a horse. Talk low and slow so you don't scare the horses, and say as little as possible before the horse runs away. But it was not such great advice for someone like me, an actor who was going to play all kinds of characters with tons of dialogue, and mostly, thankfully, with my feet planted firmly on the ground.

I am often asked what advice I have for actors starting out in this business. And for many years my answer was "Never listen to old actors like me." That was because, until John Wayne offered me his words of wisdom, I always used to ask older actors what I should do, and the only thing they ever told me was to give up.

But as I've got older, I've been reflecting on my life, as older people often do. And I've realised that, over my sixty years in the movie business and my eighty-five years of life, I have been given a lot of useful advice—by Marlene Dietrich, Tony Curtis and Laurence Olivier among many others—and I have learnt a lot of useful lessons, from my many glittering successes and my many disastrous failures. I started to think I could do a bit better than "never listen to advice." In fact, my advice would be, don't listen to *that* advice.

This book is the result of that reflection. I wanted to look back on my life from the Elephant and Castle to Hollywood, and from man-about-town Alfie to Batman's butler Alfred, with all its successes and all its failures, all its fun and all its misery and struggle, its comedy, its drama, its romance and its tragedy, and find, among it all, the lessons I've learnt and want to share, not just for aspiring movie actors but for everyone.

A few of my "lessons" are quite specific to movie acting. But I hope that most of them will speak, somehow, to most of you. You won't all have to audition for parts but in some ways life is always an audition: everyone has moments when they have to put themselves out there for what they want. You won't all have to learn lines but everyone sometimes has to make sure they're properly prepared. We all have to deal with difficult people and we all have to learn how to balance our professional and personal lives.

What you need to be a star in the movies is not that different from what you need to be a star in any other universe (it just takes a little more luck).

And if you don't give a monkey's about this old man's so-called wisdom? Well, I hope you'll still be entertained. Along the way I tell stories from my life, some old, some new, many star-studded and all entertaining, I hope, that help to tell the bigger story of how I got from where I started to where I ended up, and the mistakes I made, and the fun I had, and what I learnt along the way.

What worked for John Wayne was never going to work for me. So I don't assume that what worked for me will necessarily work for you. The world I came up in was very different from today's, and my battles as a young white working-class male movie actor in the 1950s and 1960s will not be the same as yours.

And I know that my life has been blessed with more than its fair share of good luck and good timing. As a young working-class lad in the 1960s I was in the right place at the right time. I know that. Thousands of actors out there were as good as and better than me, but didn't get the breaks. I know that too. And I know that while suddenly in the 1960s parts were being written and worlds were opening up for working-class lads like me, those breakthroughs were decades away for women and people of colour. It has taken me many decades to understand the battles—not just for the roles but for dignity and basic decency—that women have been fighting in the movies and many other industries for years, and I'm still learning.

I have been extraordinarily lucky in my personal life too, meeting my wife Shakira and having the most wonderful life with her for forty-seven years. I have been blessed with two incredible daughters, three precious grandchildren and a group of close, supportive friends.

No one can succeed in the movies or anywhere else without luck. But I haven't *just* been lucky. I've been unlucky plenty of times too. And I've never rested on my laurels. I've worked hard, learnt my craft, grabbed my opportunities and just kept on bloody going when others gave up.

Nobody has the one secret formula for success. No one can promise you riches and fame—and actually I wouldn't recommend wishing for them. A lot of actors know as much about the business as I do, and more. But if you would like a look at how one very lucky man got there, overcoming the bad luck and wringing everything he could out of the good, making tons of mistakes but trying to learn from them, doing what he loved and having a lot of fun along the way, let's get going!

PART ONE

Starting Out

I.

It Doesn't Matter Where You Start

"... you don't even see the riches you're treadin' on with your own feet"

Walter Huston to
Humphrey Bogart in *The
Treasure of the Sierra
Madre*, 1948

WHEN I LOOK AROUND me now, and look back to where I've come from, and then, just to be sure, check out the view again, I still sometimes think: What? Me? No. You're having me on. It still sometimes seems like an impossible dream. Lesson number one: I am living proof that, whatever your start in life, you can make it. Emphasis on "can"— not "will." No promises.

I was born about a million years ago in 1933, in the middle of the worst depression this country has ever known and six years before it was brought to an end by an even bigger catastrophe, the Second World War. My mother was a charlady who, though I didn't learn this until after her death, already had one son, who she was loving and caring for in secret. My father was an intelligent but completely uneducated—or undereducated, which was typical of the working class at that time—fish porter at Billingsgate market. We lived in a cramped two-room flat in a converted Victorian house in Camberwell, then one of the poorest parts of grimy, smoggy

London: three flights up from the street and five flights up from the one toilet in the garden. I suffered from rickets, a disease of poverty that causes weak bones, and I tottered up and down those stairs in surgical boots.

Three years after me came another son, Stanley, and another three years after Stanley came the Second World War. As the Blitz flattened London, my brother and I, aged three and six, were evacuated, and found ourselves at the tender mercies of separate and rather disappointing new families. Mine fed me one tin of pilchards on toast a day and kept me locked in a cupboard under the stairs when they went away for the weekends. My mother barged in and rescued me, covered with sores, as soon as the Germans stopped bombing the railway lines, but not before I'd developed lifelong claustrophobia and an absolute detestation of any cruelty to children.

I left school at sixteen with a small handful of exam passes, found and got sacked from a handful of menial office jobs, and at eighteen I got called up for National Service, where I first did my level best to help with the Allied occupation of a defeated post-war Germany and then headed off to be shot at by Communists in Korea.

Britain then was one of the most class-ridden nations in the world, and I was, I was daily informed, at the bottom of the heap. Of course there were millions of people all over the world living lives much worse than mine, but I didn't know about that. I just knew that I was poor and working-class.

In many ways it was not a great start—for anything, let alone movie stardom. But to its star— Maurice Joseph Micklewhite, as (poor sod) I was known back then—my childhood never felt like a sob story. It was what I knew, I was loved, my mother and father were great parents and even the worst of times seemed to bring me something good.

The Second World War was one of the most horrific, tragic events of the twentieth century. But for me, it was one of the greatest things that ever happened. For this scrawny six-year-old slum-dweller, it meant evacuation and escape from the Blitz—with my brother and mother the second time around. We were transported from smoke-choked London to the bliss of the Norfolk countryside where I could run around in the fresh air, nick apples and have a massive bleeding carthorse called Lottie as a pet. Like everyone else I was forced to eat organic food for five years: there were no chemicals to put on the land or in food, because they were all being used in explosives and ammunition. There was very little sugar, no sweets, no fizzy drinks, but free orange juice, cod liver oil, malt extract and vitamins. For most people rationing was terrible but for people like me the wartime diet was a great improvement. My rickets was cured and I shot up like a weed.

Because of the war I got the opportunity to take the so-called eleven-plus exam to get me a place at a good grammar school: very unusual at that time for a boy from my background. My father survived Dunkirk, El Alamein and the liberation of Rome—I still have the card he sent me for my sixth birthday from Dunkirk, and the rosary the Pope gave him in thanks in 1944—and came back to us, tireder, sadder, but a daily reminder of how lucky we were: the telegram we had dreaded every day for the six years of the war had never arrived. And when I came back to London after the war, twelve years old, still lanky but now six foot tall—already four inches taller than my father—we were rehoused in a prefab in the Elephant and Castle. It had electric light, hot water, a proper bath, a refrigerator and, best of all, an inside toilet. These were all firsts for us and it felt like luxury.

I learnt early on that everything, no matter how tragic, can have its good side for you personally. I learnt to find the good in terrible situations. Looking back I would add another lesson that I couldn't possibly have known at the time (I wish I had): if I can make it, there's hope for us all. No matter where you start in life, you can get up and out.

👓 *Learn what you can from what you get*

None of us chooses our childhood. We don't choose our families, or our circumstances, or the era we are born into. But no matter where we find ourselves, there is always something we can learn. And now, more than ever, I realise what great lessons I learnt from the good bits and the crappy bits of my early life.

My father taught me that I wanted more out of life than I was supposed to get. My mother taught me the things I needed to be able to go out and get it. Together, they provided me with a wonderful launch pad—and a wonderful grounding.

My father was a brilliant, intelligent and funny man, a hero to my brother and me. He could make a wireless from scratch out of small parts. But like many of his generation he wasn't very good at reading and writing, and because he was uneducated he was unsuited for anything but manual labour. My father was not a chirpy Cockney sparrow. He was, in truth, never truly happy. He deeply resented his situation yet felt hopeless to change it. I used to look at him and think: Blimey, with an education, what could this man have done? And then: Blimey, I need to get an education or I'll end up like him, getting up at four every morning to spend the day carting freezing cold fish about, then blowing all my wages on the horses. When my father died in St. Thomas's hospital at the age of fifty-six, I was with him. He had three shillings and eightpence in his pockets, and that was all he had to show for a lifetime of working like a beast of burden. As I walked out of the hospital ward I swore I would make something of myself, and my family would never be poor again.

My mother set me on my path to success by giving me my first acting role. At the age of three I had a regular gig in a two-hander, opening our front door to a varied cast of unsuspecting co-stars—the local debt collectors. I had only one line to deliver: "Mummy's out." Slam door, exit up the three flights of stairs back to our tiny flat.

It's a nice story and it's true. But what my mother gave me went a lot deeper than that.

My mother made me the man I am.

When my father went off to war, I was six and my brother Stanley was three. My mother didn't cry as my father got on the army truck and it drove off out of sight. She turned and looked at us and said, "Your father's gone. Now you two have to look after me."

"Right, Mum," we both said. "Of course we will. Don't you worry."

Of course it wasn't true. We couldn't possibly

look after her, and she didn't need us to: she was tough as old boots and could look after herself. Which was lucky because my father didn't come back for four years. But that solemn moment gave me an incredible sense of responsibility that stayed with me all my life. I have always wanted to take care of the people around me and always felt a terrible sense of guilt when I haven't been able to.

At the same time, Mum taught me how to relax, have fun, laugh and not take myself too seriously. She had a hard life but, unlike my father, she was not weighed down with bitterness or self-pity. She loved to laugh and she smiled her way through the humiliations of the grinding poverty that comes with being married to a gambler, six years of war waiting for the telegram boy in his silly hat and the lifelong strain of caring in secret for her beloved first child, David.

And, later, when stardom came, boy, did my mother keep me grounded.

When I had grown up (a bit) and settled down (a bit), my wife Shakira and I used to have my mother over to our house in Windsor every week for Sunday lunch. Sometimes it would be just the family and other times we would have friends there too— by this time, often very successful movie-business friends. This Sunday must have been just after I'd finished making *The Man Who Would Be King*, a

1970s escapist buddy caper set in a remote made-up land near India. The great director John Huston and the producer John Foreman, who, together with my co-star Sean Connery, had made working on that movie such a joy, were tucking into their roast dinner and my mother was earnestly engaging John Foreman on the topic of the price of milk. It was on her mind at the time, because it had just gone up by twopence, and John was agreeing with her that this was terrible. My mother always remained herself and always treated everyone the same.

She had excellent instincts about people. She knew who was a kind person and who could be trusted. And she knew that that was what was important about a person. I remember one time in the 1970s, at a party at my house that was bursting with glamorous, successful people—Peter Sellers and Liza Minnelli were there, Sean Connery, Nanette Newman, Roger Moore—my mother quietly asked me, "Who's that over there?"

I glanced across the room, packed with stars, to where she was looking and said, "That's a very famous actress, Mum. She's very famous." And I told my mum the actress's name. She was as famous as you can get, very beautiful, vivacious, the life and soul of the party.

"I don't like her," said Mum, pursing her lips. "I really don't like her."

"Why, Mum?" I said.

And my mum said, "She's spoken to everyone in this room except the old lady: me. She's not spoken to anyone old."

It's easy to get swept off your feet with the glamour of it all, unless you have some sensible people keeping you grounded.

More simply, and more importantly, my mother gave me and both of my brothers (maybe the other two even a little bit more than me because I could usually look after myself) uncomplicated, unconditional, devoted love. So much so that what I remember most clearly about my childhood Christmases is not that my father was away fighting the war, or that there were precious few presents; what I remember is my mother going at a hard-boiled sweet—the last of our Christmas rations—with a carving knife, trying to cut it in half so that neither son should feel favoured over the other. When the knife slipped and she gouged out a piece of her thumb, she disappeared for a minute, came back with it bandaged and went back to sawing away until that sweet finally surrendered to her onslaught. (My father loved me, too, but he wasn't as good at showing it.)

When you have been shown love, you can show it to others. At the beginning of her life, when I was young and broke and desperate, I wasn't always the father I wanted to be to my first daughter, Dominique. But what I have done right, as a father to Dominique and later to my second daughter Natasha, and as a grandfather to three wonderful grandchildren, I learnt from Mum and the way she offered all her three sons unconditional, unjudgemental, unfailing love.

I would even say that my mother, in a way, gave me my wife of forty-five years, Shakira. I've told the story many times of how I first stumbled across, pursued and fell hopelessly in love with Shakira, and Shakira has begged me not to tell it again here. So if you don't know this incredible, unlikely story of the greatest run of luck I ever had, I'm very sorry but you'll have to find it somewhere else. But not so many people know the story of how this stunning, poised, intelligent woman fell for little old me. I had always assumed it was my smooth Cockney charm and suave good looks that had swept Shakira off her feet, until one day I was standing at the door eavesdropping on an interview my wife was doing for a newspaper. "What first attracted you to Michael?" the journalist asked, and I heard her reply, "It was the way he treated his mother."

Most successful people will have a story to tell about a great teacher, and I am no exception. The headmistress at the village school I attended in

Norfolk was an intimidating and fierce-looking woman, about sixty years old, called Miss Linton. She had an unusual haircut for a woman—similar to my father's, I thought—was unmarried, smoked 100 cigarettes a day and was extremely tough with us children. Except that after a while her attitude towards me softened. She started to take a close interest in me, gave me special lessons, guided my reading, taught me to play poker to improve my maths and eventually got me through the scholarship exam for grammar school. I never saw her happier than the day she came rushing across the village green to tell me I had passed: the first child from the village school ever to do so.

Miss Linton was probably the first person I loved outside my own family. Initially strange and frightening, and ultimately an inspirational figure who changed the course of my life, she was an early study in character for me. Could she have guessed that the most important lesson she taught the boy she treated like a son was that people are not always as they first appear?

I got to grammar school but didn't make the most of it. I hated the school I was sent to once the war was over (and I'm sure the feeling was mutual) and played truant whenever I could. My main education from that point forward came from two sources: books and the movies. Books like Norman

Mailer's *The Naked and the Dead* and James Jones's *From Here to Eternity*, and movies like *The Treasure of the Sierra Madre, The Maltese Falcon* and *The African Queen*, directed by John Huston, allowed me to escape from the grim, depressing reality of everyday post-war life, and reassured me that the world was bigger than the few bits I could see over the rubble of the bombsites and through the thick London smog. I can't recommend bunking off school to anyone who wants to get on in life, but if you are going to do it, you couldn't find two more richly educational surrogates than the cinema and the public library.

The Elephant (which is what anyone local called the Elephant and Castle, ideally accompanied by a hard, unblinking stare for extra menace) was a tough neighbourhood. I learnt from an early age the importance of having friends who've got your back.

Down the Elephant in the 1950s the most dangerous gangs were the spivs, and after that, the Teddy Boys, who were the children of the spivs. These gangs were viciously violent, hot-tempered and dangerous. As a skinny pale fifteen-year-old what could I do? Round my way, if you were on your own you had no chance. I had to join a gang myself. In my gang we were mostly very funny and very calm. We didn't go out looking for trouble.

I was reminded of this in 2009 when I was back in the Elephant, making a film called *Harry Brown* and getting to know some of the local young men, who started off hanging around the shoot and ended up actually in the movie, ably directed by talented young first-time director Daniel Barber. I was surprised and gratified that these lads were prepared to talk to an old man like me about their lives, and as they did, it dawned on me how much bleaker life had become on my home patch. Our prefab house had been small but what there was of it was ours: we had a little garden of our own, our own fence, our own front door. Behind it there had been a loving family and a decent education. These kids lived in dilapidated high-rise blocks full of dangerous corners and alleyways, many had difficult family backgrounds and had given up on school, and in place of the alcohol and fist-fights of my youth there were drugs, guns and knives. Worst of all, there was nothing for them to do and nowhere for them to go.

What a lot of people don't realise is that young lads in gangs, we are not there to attack you. We are there, most of us, so that no one will attack us. Young people who join gangs are not bad lads: they are making a rational choice to protect themselves from harm.

I was also, without really knowing it, gaining some useful skills. I was learning to get along by performing: acting like I was tough and wasn't afraid, when I was actually always afraid and not tough at all. And I was learning to watch and listen: to observe people carefully for a fast take on their character and mood. Malevolent? Trustworthy? Volatile?

My gang dropped me during my years as an out-of-work actor: I couldn't afford to get my round in the pub, and if I was an actor I was probably a poof, so I was out. By then I was part of a new gang of other out-of-work actors, writers and musicians. No one was coming at us with knives but we had each other's backs in different ways. Now, in my ninth decade, my friends are dropping like flies, and having their back more often than not means turning up to their memorial. The point is, whether you call them a gang, your mates or your comrades-in-arms, no one gets very far without friends—people who like you for who you really are, and who have your back. (Or if they do, they don't have much fun on the way.)

At the age of eighteen, along with all the other kids in my gang, I was called up for two years of National Service. In my case this meant two years as an infantryman in the British Army.

If my mother had started to make me into a man when my father went off to fight in the Second

World War, and my teenage years of weaving a safe path through the Elephant had added street smarts, then National Service finished the job when it sent me off to fight in the Korean War. National Service was, at the time, the worst experience of my life. In the warm comfort of hindsight, it was still the worst bloody experience of my life up to that point and at any time since. But I can also see that it was one of the most valuable.

Basic training was an exercise in physical and mental mortification. I don't remember ever walking anywhere during those first eight weeks: we ran, we hauled ourselves around assault courses, we marched, we drilled, we ran some more. If we were awake and we weren't doing any of those things, we were cleaning and polishing our ill-fitting uniforms and obsolete bits of kit. They might not fit, they might malfunction, but at least they were spotless and gleaming. We were strongly encouraged to do all of this by the humourless roaring sergeants, whose weary task it was to toughen up this assorted ragbag of Britain's finest.

As part of the Allied occupation force in post-war Germany, I was on almost continuous punishment duty for the offence of not being illiterate, which rare accomplishment I used to learn the army rules and, more to the point, how far we could push things and still stay within them. My life was made a misery with peeling potatoes, doing guard duty while everyone else went into town, and once being made to scrape clean the floorboards of the guard room using a box of old-fashioned razor blades.

How I yearned for those potatoes and those razor blades as I sat in my First World War–style trench in Korea, accompanied by several hundred of the world's most confident and ingenious rats, and facing off over the 38th Parallel around two million very pissed-off Chinese.

My fear, when I was sent on active service to Korea, was that I might be a coward. I might run away. I did believe several times that I might be about to die: on guard duty on my first night on the front line; under sniper fire; on encountering a six-foot snake. In those situations I found that I was not a coward. I was scared witless, but I was not a coward. No doubt that was partly my military training. And partly my tough bugger of a father, who, by teaching me boxing down on his knees, and ending every fight by knocking me over and announcing, "You've lost," had always encouraged me to fight my corner. But I think it was something inside me as well. I just hadn't known it was there.

One black, humid, mosquito-infested night, it was my turn to go out on patrol in no man's land, with two mates and an officer. Halfway across the unoccupied territory, we smelt garlic, which struck terror into our hearts. The Chinese soldiers chewed garlic like the Americans chewed gum, and the smell was always the first sign you were in trouble. It took quite a lot of effort years later to eat food with garlic in it. It was the same with olive oil, which my mother used to put in our ears to get rid of wax. The idea of putting it on a salad and eating it was disgusting to me then, but not now. I've become civilised, and deaf.

Anyway, back to certain death. When my four-man patrol was ambushed in no man's land that night, I experienced not fear but anger, white-hot anger, at the thought that I was going to be killed in this terrible stinking place for no good reason, before I'd even had the chance to live, before I had realised even one of my dreams. I decided that if I was going to die, I was going to take as many people as possible with me. I was going to fight my way out. The others agreed. We charged towards the enemy.

The enemy, it turned out, wasn't there. We and they charged around each other all night, and eventually the four of us in my patrol found a safe route back to our line. Our faces were unrecognisable, puffed up with mosquito bites. We were ugly and exhausted. But that night has always been important to me. I had faced what I thought was certain death and not been a coward. And I had learnt something else about myself that would stay with me for the rest of my life: if anyone wants to come for me, they had better be prepared to pay the price, because I'll be fighting as I go down. I don't wish anyone any harm. But if you're going to try to frighten me or threaten me—if you want to come for me—be ready to pay, because I'll make it costly for you.

When our year in Korea was up, we marched out as our replacements were being marched in. They were nineteen years old—only a year younger than us—but as we marched past them, I looked into their faces, and I looked into my mates' faces. We looked five years, maybe ten years older. We'd grown up. We'd been tested. We knew now what life was about. And me, I had faced death and I felt lucky to be alive, and more determined than ever to make something of my life.

What I learnt from National Service was: do anything to avoid being an infantry soldier in a war. Even if you're lucky enough to survive unscathed it will be absolutely, unimaginably terrible. On the other hand, I have found it pretty easy to be happy since then: once you've been on manoeuvres in Korea, everything else seems like quite a lot of fun. The rest of my life, I've lived every bloody moment from the moment I open my eyes until the time my head hits the pillow.

War is terrible and disgusting, and I wouldn't

wish any young person to have to experience it. I wouldn't ask anyone to go anywhere or do anything that would get them killed or wounded. But I do believe in the value of peacetime National Service. Six months of hard work and discipline—running miles in the pouring rain, assaulting assault courses, polishing filthy equipment to maniacal standards, following orders and learning how to defend your country—instil values and a sense of belonging that stay with you for the rest of your life. I know that makes me sound old-fashioned. But for young people now, with most decent jobs needing a good level of education, and with phones and iPads there to distract them all the time, I think discipline and a sense of purpose are more important than they have ever been.

👓 Forget rich and famous: find what you love

This might sound funny coming from me. But to anyone who's trying to become rich and famous, my advice is: don't.

When I was a young lad that was never my goal. The screen idols I worshipped at the cinema every Saturday morning—Marlon Brando, Spencer Tracy, Cary Grant, Clark Gable and my biggest hero

Humphrey Bogart—were handsome and beautiful with broad shoulders, sun tans and gleaming white teeth, the sophisticated movie-god occupants of a glamorous heaven called Hollywood, and I was a gangly working-class boy with a big nose.

With my appearance and my accent, I knew for sure I would never be a star. That world was distant, unreachable. In those days, in the 1940s and 1950s, your accent didn't just tell where you came from, it told where you were going to, and if you had a Cockney accent like mine, that was nowhere.

I didn't dream of becoming rich and famous. That wasn't my goal. But I did, at a young age, find something I loved to do: acting. In a life full of good fortune this was the biggest piece of good luck I ever had.

I found acting through my other great love. Aged fourteen, spotty, skinny and horny, I saw a group of beautiful unattainable girls through a window at my youth club, Clubland, an incredible all-mod-cons facility in the Walworth Road built out of nothing and run by the Reverend Jimmy Butterworth. As I was gazing, rapt, at this gaggle of lovelies, the door I was leaning on fell open and I found myself making a perfect (and perfectly humiliating) pratfall entrance into the drama club. Once I'd pulled myself together it came to me in a flash. I had stumbled into a two-birds-with-one-stone situation. I could learn to act so that I could get to Hollywood, and in the meantime, perhaps if I played enough love scenes I might somehow get my first kiss. So I came to acting for all the wrong reasons, but once I'd found it, I never looked back.

Trying to describe why you love doing what you love doing is a bit like trying to describe why you love who you love, or why your favourite colour is blue. It feels obvious but also inexpressible why aquamarine is the most pleasing shade, and that your beloved is the most amazing person you have ever been lucky enough to meet. In the same way, to me it feels both unquestionably true and also inexplicable how acting is the most fun you can have without breaking any laws.

In my very first role for the Clubland youth club, I played a robot who had one line. It was a modest role and one that the sarcastic and rather cruel reviewer noted I was well suited for. But I still remember the excitement of putting on the show, and the tremendous sense of achievement when it was all over. I got the same feelings in every show I put on, every movie I made. It's about working together to create something. And it's about communication and control. If I can say something and make an audience laugh, say something else and make them cry, it's just a stunning sensation. If I can make an audience know about, or worry about, or love things they didn't know about, or worry about, or love before—help them to discover life—that's stunning to me too.

Plus, I couldn't ever bleeding think of anything else I could do.

But I never set out to be rich and famous. Quite the opposite. Knowing I would never be a star, I just set out to enjoy myself and be the best actor I could possibly become in my own small world. Not a star, not richer or more famous than anyone else, just the best I could be. If rewards came, that would be wonderful, but I wasn't doing it for that. I loved it, it was fun and it was better than working in a factory.

Forget rich and famous. It's not a career. It is—for the tiny number of people who ever achieve it—the miraculous result of a lot of hard work combined with tremendous good luck. For very many people, it doesn't even turn out to be all it's cracked up to be. It's not something to aim for.

Instead, my biggest piece of advice to anyone just starting out—or to anyone who feels like they've taken a wrong turn along the way—is this: find something you want to do and learn how to do it really well. Take what you've got and make the most of it. Learn how to do something. Whatever it is you would choose to do for nothing. Whatever it is that, when you're doing it, makes you feel amazing and most yourself. Throw yourself into it. Challenge yourself to be the best you can be. We can't all be famous actors. But if you can find something you love, and if that something will also pay the bills, you will be on your way to your own personal paradise.

2.

Auditioning for Life

"All I ever wanted for you was to go out in the world and chase your dreams. Find adventure, fall in love, take risks. That's all I wanted for you."

Mr. Morgan's Last Love,
2013

FOR THE FIRST NINE years of my professional acting career, it felt more like purgatory than paradise. I never fell out of love with acting—and I never have. But I struggled to make what I loved pay the bills. Every small success seemed to be followed by two desperately disappointing failures (a pattern that some might argue I continued to follow through my whole career).

By the time I was thirty years old, I must have done seven or eight hundred auditions, and played more than a hundred different parts in repertory theatre, another hundred small parts on TV, thirty one-line movie roles and a couple of walk-on parts in the West End.

Did I get good at auditioning? Or did I just do so much of it that I was bound to catch a break? I don't know. Here's what I do know about auditions, though. And don't take it too literally. If you're an actor and you really do have an audition, then great. But what goes for an audition goes for any area of life you want to impress in. There are a lot of situa-

tions in life where you have to put yourself out there
to get something you want.

👓 *You are always auditioning*

If you only think you're auditioning when you're in
the room with the casting director, you're missing
half of it. You're auditioning when you're checking
in with the receptionist, when you're sitting in the
waiting area, when you're grabbing a cup of coffee.

In fact, whenever you're in any public space,
you're auditioning. You never know who's watching
your performance. At the gym? You're being audi-
tioned by your instructor. He knows that the guy
sweating away on the next bike has a flat share with
an up-and-coming script writer. Walking your dog?
That woman with the out-of-control Border Col-
lie is checking you out. She's an associate producer
for a major production company. Trying to decide
whether to intervene in a worrying altercation on
the top deck of the bus? The frightened young bus
driver, whose career is about to take a sharp turn up-
wards, will always remember that day.

This may all sound far-fetched but I can assure
you it's not. My friend Sean Connery had never
acted a day in his life until he got discovered lifting
weights in a gym by a casting director looking

for some slightly more convincing sailors than the usual chorus line for *South Pacific.* When I was shooting the comedy-heist *Gambit* with Shirley MacLaine, Universal had just started its famous studio tours, and in those days the tourists were allowed onto the actual sets. Every day a tour bus would pull up, tourists would pile out and the driver would try to convince any actors who hadn't scurried out of sight, like gazelles on a safari, to sign autographs.

One driver was particularly clever at timing his stops. It was annoying, but I also admired his initiative. I knew he had a job to do and my better nature prevailed. I decided to make him look good and, instead of trying to avoid his tour party, I signed every autograph and posed for every picture, and got to know him a little. And who did the bus driver turn out to be? Mike Ovitz, then a student but later the founder, then chairman, of CAA, the world's leading talent agency and one of the most powerful people in Hollywood. And when, working as a doorman at a dodgy hotel in Victoria, I rescued a frightened prostitute from the attentions of a drunk and violent punter (I knocked him out but forgot about his five friends, who proceeded to return the favour), who could have known that the hotel owner's son, Barry Krost, would become a Hollywood agent and a great friend, who would, years later, put together the deal to make *Get Carter*?

Not an actor? Doesn't matter. Whatever your role is, perform it as though the girl on the checkout, the young woman making your coffee, or, yes, even the guy at the other end of the line trying to fix your computer, is your dream boss, dream date, dream client. It will make you a better person. And sometimes, just sometimes, they really are.

Know what you convey

If you are always putting yourself out there, always alert to a possible opening, always focused on your goal, always performing, that's a start. But do you know what other people are seeing when they watch your performance? Do you have a good sense of what you convey? Do you know your strengths, and play them up?

I was a Cockney lad and I knew nobody was going to look at me and see an actor, so I decided to invent myself and create a readily recognisable image. It started with the glasses. No aspiring actors wore glasses back then, but I actually needed them to see, so I decided I would be the actor who wore glasses. Great big black ones so you couldn't miss them. Then David Bailey took a brilliant photo of me, with my big black glasses on and a cigarette dangling from my mouth. It wouldn't be now, but in those days that was considered the height of cool. I became the cool working-class actor who wore glasses. Most importantly though, word got around that I was hard-working and reliable. I was that easy-to-work-with cool working-class guy in glasses. It was the truth but I tended it and played up to it, so nobody could miss it.

Later on, I wanted people to see beyond the Cockney (though I tried to hang on to the cool). I kept reinventing myself, kept reassessing my strengths. Maybe you're trying to get noticed at work. Maybe you're trying to get noticed by a special someone. Whatever your walk of life, at work or in your personal life, don't let your image imprison you. Don't let how others see you decide what you can be. But be realistic: know what you convey, and use that to your advantage.

You never know where your break will come from

There is no one sure route to success. No single rule to follow, no single book to read, no one bus stop to get spotted at. Instead success comes, for the lucky few it comes to, from a magical mix of talent, hard work, determination and sheer dumb luck. You never know where your break will come from so you have to be on high alert for it all the time. And don't expect it to look like a bolt from the blue. Big breaks are rare. Much more common is a series of little breaks, each one a small step on the staircase to success.

My first crucial break came from a little old man in a butter factory. When I came out of the army I was more determined than ever to follow my dream of being an actor, but I had no idea how to go about it. I sat around my parents' prefab, getting underfoot and trying to work out how to get onto the first rung of a non-existent ladder. After a while I realised I had to get a job and, since opportunities were few and far between, I accepted that my first step to stardom would have to be a job mixing butter.

One day I was heaving crates of butter into the vat, thinking this wasn't much improvement on heaving crates of cold fish, like my father, and the old man working alongside me said, "What the hell are you doing here? A young lad like you. What is it you want to be?"

And I told him. "Well," I said, "I want to be an actor." I braced myself for the usual response but instead of cracking up he just nodded, like this was a normal thing for someone like me to want. "But I don't know how," I said. I had never even heard of RADA (the Royal Academy of Dramatic Art) or the Actors Studio, never mind knowing anything about how to get there.

"Well," the old man said, "I'm going to tell you." I looked at him in astonishment.

"You want to get the *Stage*," he said. "Go down to Solosy's, the newsagent on the Charing Cross Road. They stock it. Look at the back page. That's where they advertise for actors." He told me that his daughter was a semi-professional singer and got a lot of work that way.

That Saturday I was outside Solosy's when it opened. I bought the *Stage* and there on the back page was an advert for an assistant stage manager (plus minor acting roles) with a small repertory theatre company in Horsham, Sussex. Applicants should send a photo.

The old man in the butter factory was probably just passing the time of day but he had given me a piece of advice I desperately needed and set me on my way. It was my first big break and it led me to my first and perhaps my easiest ever audition, down in Horsham, one week later.

I was a twenty-year-old strapping ex-soldier, six foot two with curly blond hair and a tan I had acquired on the boat back from Korea; in the photo I'd hastily had taken, I appeared to be wearing lipstick. The owner of the company, Mr. Alwyn D. Fox, was about fifty years old, small and camp. He stood with one hand on his hip and the other on his face, looked me over in the way I was used to looking over girls and screamed, "Edgar!" In came Edgar, a smaller, camper, more delicate version of Mr. Fox. Edgar stood next to Mr. Fox and adopted an identical pose. "Will he do, do you think?"

"Mm," said Edgar finally. "He'll do."

My worst audition? From a large and strong field of competitors I would have to pick my audition for the theatre play of *Alfie* in 1963. I wanted it too much and I got very nervous because of that and because I was overawed by being in the West End. I completely screwed up the line. So that was it. I was distraught. The man they cast was a wonderful classical actor called John Neville, a lovely guy with the most beautiful classical voice. He sounded like John Gielgud.

Instead my incomparable agent Dennis Selinger persuaded me to take a much less sought-after part as the lead in a cheap but very good theatre production of a Theatre of the Absurd play called *Next Time I'll Sing to You*, about a man who didn't speak for forty-two years. It wasn't *Alfie* and the pay was terrible, but Dennis's calculation was that this play would attract critical attention and get me noticed. As usual he was absolutely right.

One night the film star and movie producer Stanley Baker was in the audience. He knew me a little from when I had played a bit part with eight lines to say in a movie called *A Hill in Korea* in 1956. Stanley came to see me backstage after the show and asked me whether I would like to screen test for the part of an insubordinate but heroic Cockney, Private Henry Hook, in his movie *Zulu*, about the 1879 battle of Rorke's Drift between the British Army and the Zulu nation. I had only played one-day parts in movies before: this was an enormous opportunity for me.

But when I turned up at the Prince of Wales Theatre the next morning, the director, Cy Endfield, was apologetic. He had already given the part to my friend James Booth, who, I had to admit, was an excellent choice. It was a punch to the gut but by now I had pretty strong gut muscles from all the previous punches I'd taken. I held myself together and walked away. And *that* was when I got my break.

The bar at the Prince of Wales Theatre is very long, which is fortunate for me because that's how I became a movie star. Just as I had reached the end of it and was about to get out of there, and go away to curl up and quietly die, Cy called me back.

Until that point in my career, everybody in the business used to say, "Oh, Michael Caine. He's no leading man, of course, he's a Cockney, but if you have a juicy little Cockney role he'll do you a lovely job with it." I'd cultivated the image and it had its uses, but it was holding me back.

But Cy said, "Michael, you don't look like a Cockney, you look like an officer. Can you do a posh British accent?" I told him I'd been in rep, doing fifty plays a year and every accent from peasant to baronet. "That's the easiest one of all," I said, fingers crossed behind my back.

"Will you come and do a screen test with Stanley on Friday?" asked Cy.

"Yes," I said, to the most unnecessary question I had ever been asked.

A screen test is the movie industry's own special and terrifying way of assessing your on-camera potential because it's impossible to judge just by looking at someone. You have to put them to work in front of a camera and see whether the magic happens: whether millions of people are going to want to spend their time and their money listening to that voice, watching that face. They put the camera in your face and do a close-up. They make you turn sideways for a profile. They give you a key scene of tricky dialogue and have you play it with another actor reading in the other parts. It all comes down to what you look like on camera, how your voice sounds, how relaxed and natural you seem and whether you have that indescribable, unlearnable, instantly recognisable thing we call star quality. And if you've got it, you've got it.

Beyond chasing Chinese soldiers through no man's land, my screen test for the part of the aristocratic and effete Lieutenant Gonville Bromhead in *Zulu* was the single most nerve-racking thing I've ever done. Stanley and Cy could not have been kinder or more patient but it was a complete disaster. I did not ooze star quality. I oozed sweat, panic and abject terror.

That weekend Cy came up to me at a party. "I've seen the test," he told me. "And it's the worst I've ever seen." Time to tense those stomach muscles again. "But I don't know, Michael, I think there's something there. You've got the part." He walked away and, before I could instruct my stomach muscles to stand down, I had thrown up all over my shoes.

I felt like a champion, despite my ruined shoes. Somehow, I had kept riding the punches. It's the same in any enterprise, whatever you're trying to accomplish. You never know when your moment will arrive, and you don't want to be on the floor and out for the count when it does.

Things were finally looking up. I'd done a starring role in a TV play, a starring theatre role, and now I had a big movie role. But it took another year, and the release of *Zulu*, for me to catch my next break.

It was 1964 and London was in full swing. Stars were falling from the skies like rain. I was having dinner with my friend Terence Stamp in the Pickwick, a club-cum-restaurant on Great Newport Street that always seemed to be full of beautiful and talented people, and was *the* "in" place at the time, when a waiter came over and gave me a piece of paper. It was a note from the Bond film producer Harry Saltzman, asking me to go and have coffee with him and his family when I'd finished my meal. My friend Sean Connery was playing Bond by this time: he was the only Brit of my generation to have made it in Hollywood. I thought I was going to get a part in a James Bond film.

I joined Harry at his table, my heart beating wildly. His wife told me that they had just come from seeing *Zulu*, then Harry announced, "We all agreed you could be a big star."

I blushed and my heart beat even faster. I maybe managed to blurt out, "Thank you."

Harry abruptly changed topic. Had I read a book by Len Deighton called *The Ipcress File*?

"Yes," I said, which was true—I was in the middle of reading it right then. It was about a spy, but the spy was the opposite of James Bond. He was ordinary and unglamorous. I was made for the part.

"I've just bought the movie rights to it and I'd like you to play the lead."

"Yes," I managed, trying to look as though I got offers like that every day.

"And would you like a seven-year contract?"

"Yes," I managed again. In a daze I stumbled back to my table and tried to explain what had happened to an astonished Terry. In the ten minutes I had been gone I had scored my first lead role in a movie and, not that I knew it then, it was the role that made me into a British—though not yet a Hollywood—star.

Life offers you breaks all the time. Occasionally they're big movie-mogul-in-a-restaurant–style breaks. More often they are lower-key, more subtle. Be ready. Recognise them. Grab them. Use them.

👓 Be lucky: be prepared

Admittedly, my timing could not have been better. The late 1950s and early 1960s were a vibrant, exciting time to be young and working-class in Britain. My generation was inventing a whole new technicolour world, overturning the dull and dreary post-war status quo, and there were opportunities for people like me—not just in theatre and film, but in fashion, music, art, food, literature, politics—that there had never been before.

Young people, whose childhoods had been the

depression, the Blitz, conscription and rationing, were listening to Khrushchev, the leader of the Soviet Union, telling them that he had an atomic bomb and we could all be dead in four minutes, and deciding they might as well have a good time. The working class was standing up and saying, "We are here, this is our society, and we're not going away." And that's how and why the sixties were born. Everyone I knew seemed to become a household name.

If you danced at the Ad Lib club just behind the Empire Cinema on Leicester Square, as I did, the Rolling Stones and the Beatles might be grooving around next to you. David Bailey would be in the corner, romancing Jean Shrimpton. In another corner Roman Polanski was with Sharon Tate.

My flatmate was Terence Stamp. My barber was Vidal Sassoon. My tailor was Douglas Hayward, the tailor to the 1960s and such a star in his field that he ended up making Ralph Lauren's suits. When I played a bit part in *Dixon of Dock Green* I was paired with an unknown actor called Donald Sutherland. When I understudied another unknown actor making his West End debut in one of the first British plays about ordinary soldiers, Willis Hall's *The Long and the Short and the Tall,* it was Peter O'Toole. The play made him a star and I took it on tour while he went off to become T. E. Lawrence in David Lean's

Lawrence of Arabia, the start of a towering theatrical and movie-making career.

Even the failed actors became household names. When the rest of us were still out of work and broke, we used to pass the time in the basement café of the Arts Theatre, just off Leicester Square. They would let you sit there all day over one cup of tea. One afternoon I was sitting in this warm haven for the destitute with two other broke actor friends. One of them, John, was particularly down. He had just been fired from a very low-standard repertory theatre and was humiliated and unhappy. He announced that he was going to give it all up and had already written a play instead. "What's it called?" I asked.

"*Look Back in Anger*," he replied.

"I'm writing a play as well," said our other friend, an actor called David Baron. "And you can be in it, Michael. Only I'm not going to write it under my acting name. I'm going to use my real name."

"What's that, David?"

"Harold Pinter."

"Well, good luck to both of you," I said. I didn't hold out much hope for either of them.

As a child and a young man, I hadn't seen a single British film about the working class, or about private soldiers. Although I didn't really go to the theatre, there were no plays about the working class either. At that time, the only working-class British actor who had ever made it in Hollywood was Charlie Chaplin. And how had he done it? He was lucky enough to be around in the days of silent films when it didn't matter what you sounded like. Oh, and Cary Grant: but he had a Bristol accent and somehow, because it sounded quite American, that worked too. Also not to be forgotten, just a few years younger than me, there was Richard Burton. He was as genuinely working-class as you could get: the twelfth of thirteen children, son of a Welsh coal miner, his mother died when he was just two years old. Richard broke through, all right, thanks to talent, hard work and, of course, some great pieces of luck, but he had to transform himself into a great classical orating theatre actor, like Olivier or Gielgud, to do it.

But in the late 1950s and the 1960s (the 1960s really started in the late 1950s), writers were writing plays and films about the working class: pieces like John Osborne's *Look Back in Anger*, Shelagh Delaney's *A Taste of Honey* and Alan Sillitoe's *Saturday Night and Sunday Morning* that collectively became known as kitchen-sink dramas, and Harold Pinter's works, including *The Room*, with, as promised, a part for me, and his better-known later plays, *The Birthday Party* and *The Caretaker*. A cohort of (male) working-class actors—people like Roger Moore,

Sean Connery, Peter O'Toole and me—found enough interesting parts to break through.

Until the 1960s, movie stars had to be superior, distant and unreachable. In the 1960s, we had to be the opposite: the audience had to believe that if they happened to meet Roger, Sean or me in the pub, we would buy them a pint and we'd have a good laugh. In the 1960s, the working class stopped being invisible and pitiable and became cool and modern. That suited me much better.

So I was lucky. And "be lucky" is, I realise, not that useful as a life lesson. But I've heard it said that luck favours the prepared and I believe it.

So be prepared. And I always was. For me that meant, specifically, knowing my lines. Know your lines until you could come out of unconsciousness and say them, until saying them is no harder than reciting the alphabet or counting to ten. Could you say your lines while half your brain is doing something else, like cooking an omelette or packing a suitcase, or chasing someone down the street? If not, you're unlikely to be able to get them out at your audition, when half your mind will be frozen with nerves and the other half trying to register the names of the people who have just introduced themselves to you.

And don't say them in your head or mouth them silently. (This is an acting tip I picked up from the great theatre and screen actor Laurence Olivier.) If there's a tongue-twister in there, or a combination of consonants you find difficult, you won't find it unless you say the lines out loud. Ever had that feeling where the sound of your own voice takes you by surprise, and seems unreal, unconvincing? Don't let that happen in an audition, an interview, a date, a sales pitch. Practise until it sounds natural. Practise until it *is* natural. If you can't convince yourself, how are you going to convince anyone else?

Don't look in the mirror, though. That's only a useful preparation if you're going to be playing identical twins. I don't like having someone else read the other part to me either. I like to keep the dialogue fresh enough so that when I hear the lines in the audition I can react to them as though I'm hearing them said for the first time, the way you would in a real conversation. But I do familiarise myself with those lines because they provide the logic behind what my character is saying and thinking.

And think of all those auditions when you didn't get called back and all those walk-on parts (or the job interviews or client pitches where they decided to go another way, or the first dates that went nowhere) not as failures but as part of your preparation. Because luck favours the focused, the hard grafters and the rubber-ball resilient. Most of my luck happened when someone saw me playing one role and offered me another: maybe slightly bigger or slightly better.

A lot had to go right for me to get that part in *Zulu*. The movie producer Stanley Baker had to spot me in the theatre. He had to remember me from my eight-line part in *A Hill in Korea* (a part I'd only got thanks to my experience in Korea: I was also supposed to be a "technical adviser," although no one ever took a blind bit of notice of anything I said). The part he wanted me for had to go to someone else. I had to be able to do a posh English accent. The director had to be American: no English director would have considered me to play the part of an officer—not through malice; it was just the class-based way everyone thought. The bar had to be long enough and I had to walk back down it with some semblance of dignity. Luck? Or preparation, focus, hard work and resilience?

A different series of things had to go right for me to get the lead in *Alfie*. First, Bill Naughton had to write this part of a lifetime for a young working-class British actor: a cheeky, charming, irresponsible and ultimately rather sad and lonely lad-about-town. (And let me put something to rest once and for all: I am not Alfie. We were both Cockney lads and we both like women but that is where the similarities end. How he treats women is the exact opposite of how I would treat a woman. That wasn't me: that was acting.)

Then, once the (not-so-successful) play got made into a film, half a dozen people had to turn the part down. Terence Stamp was offered it first, but he had played the part on Broadway, and although he had been great, the play had flopped. He turned it down. Then Anthony Newley, James Booth and Laurence Harvey turned it down. Eventually Jonny Gilbert, the son of the director Lewis Gilbert, suggested me. A brilliant example of a friend who had my back, by the way. Lewis didn't really know who I was but Jonny took him to see me as Harry Palmer in *The Ipcress File*, my first lead role in a movie. That was how I got cast in *Alfie*, which was an enormous hit in Britain and Europe, got me my first Academy Award nomination, and was the first of my films to get a release in the United States. (This required me to redo 124 lines of dialogue. The Americans would never have understood my Cockney accent, a point that my American co-star Shelley Winters confirmed to me. She told me she hadn't understood a word I'd said during the shoot and had resorted to watching my lips to know when to come in.) Yes, a lot of luck, but I like to think that wasn't the whole story.

I have also come to understand that my other enormous piece of good luck during these early years was that, while I had a lot of truly terrible and mortifying auditions, I was never put in the humiliating, frightening position of being asked for, or even forced into, sex in return for a part. There was no casting couch for me, no sexual negotiation, no harassment. No one ever even approached me, and I was always treated with respect. It used to go a bit quiet when I took my trousers off in the communal men's dressing room in the repertory theatre at Horsham, but that was the extent of it.

I always knew (or thought I knew) about the "casting couch" but, to my regret and shame, I never thought too hard about it. My own battle was against a certain snobbery about my background and my accent, but I never had to think about the ugly kinds of battles others were fighting. I think, on reflection, I got the long straw. And I hope for the sake of today's young people, trying to make their way in the world, that both the snobbery of the 1950s and the sexual power plays of more recent times can be consigned permanently to the past.

3.

Using the Difficulty

"We only ever told each other the good things."

Youth, 2015

THERE CAME A POINT, somewhere between *Zulu* and *Alfie*, where I didn't have to audition any more. But if you think this all sounds easy, or like I had a gilded path to success, then that's just the way I told it. It wasn't and I didn't. Those first years of my career were brutal.

After a few happy months playing small parts and making the tea in Horsham Rep, I collapsed on stage during a Saturday matinee performance of *Wuthering Heights* and was diagnosed with a rare form of cerebral malaria, a parting gift from the Korean mosquitoes. By the time I had recovered, several weeks later, forty pounds lighter, my face tinged yellow, I would only have been good for horror plays, but it didn't matter: the company had folded.

I headed back to Solosy's, found a new job as juvenile lead in rep in Lowestoft and, way too young at twenty-two, married the female lead, a beautiful and talented actress called Patricia Haines. We had met just a few weeks earlier. What can I say? Lowestoft is a romantic city. I was desperately in love but much too immature for the responsibility, and the marriage was a disaster from the outset. We left Lowestoft for a small flat in Brixton, where we both struggled to find acting work, and argued about how to support ourselves. I eventually took on a series of soul-destroying menial jobs while Patricia pursued her acting career.

Meanwhile my heart was breaking in a different way, watching my father, who was only fifty-five, fading away in agony from liver cancer. These were tough years, and by the time Patricia's and my daughter Dominique was born, our marriage was all but broken. My beautiful child was just eight months old when I walked out. Pat took Dominique back to her parents in Sheffield, who took on the job of raising her (and did a superb job). My sense of guilt, inadequacy and desperation was intense. I moved back to the prefab with Mum and came very close to a breakdown.

I was always on the edge of destitution. Here's the list of dead-end jobs I worked: I washed dishes, I worked in a steelyard, I packed laundry, I worked pneumatic drills on the roads and I was a night porter for a very dodgy hotel catering to a lot of couples called Smith in Victoria. In my worst moments I went on the dole (the last time, Sean Connery was two guys in front of me in the queue). I owed small sums of money all over London and often had to dash across the street to avoid my creditors. I came perilously close to going to jail for getting behind with my maintenance payments for Dominique. The whole time I was going to auditions.

At one point, my agent, Pat Larthe, unwittingly nearly finished me off when she secured an interview for me with the chief casting director of Associated British Pictures, which was then one of the biggest movie companies in Britain and, like the Hollywood studios of the time, kept a number of actors under contract. Robert Lennard was a man with the power to solve my financial problems and make my career in one stroke, and his pleasant fatherly manner made what he had to say all the more devastating. He told me it was a tough business, which I knew. He told me he had a son who looked like me, which I didn't know. Then he said, "My son is an accountant and he has more chance of success in this business than you do." I sat there numb but smiling. He went on, "I've got to be frank with you, Michael, I know this business well and you have no future in it at all. Give it up, Michael." I kept smiling through my fury, thanked him for his advice and walked out more determined than ever to succeed.

I took to hanging around a casting agency just off Trafalgar Square, waiting to see if I could get the odd walk-on part—play, TV, film, whatever I could get. It was the kind of place where if you fitted the policeman's uniform the film company had in its wardrobe, you got the part. It was crushingly soul-sapping.

In summary, there were more knockbacks than call-backs. More knockbacks than you could shake a stick at. And the thing is, I was not particularly unlucky. My friends were in similar positions, or worse. My oldest and dearest childhood friend Paul Challen, who had grown up in an orphanage and never been strong in the first place, had his acting career cut short when he succumbed to tuberculosis. Two good friends, Jonny Charlesworth and Peter Myers, committed suicide, unable to cope with the financial and emotional toll of the constant rejection. The other people hanging around with me waiting for work included Sean Connery, Richard Harris, Terence Stamp, Peter O'Toole, Albert Finney, Tom Courtenay, and many others who found it too tough and turned their backs on their dreams.

Everyone had it tough. Some paths were easier than others, but one thing is for sure: there was no overnight success. There is no such thing as an overnight success. Behind every apparent overnight success is some poor bastard who's been slogging away, unnoticed and unappreciated, for years.

Acting is a notoriously difficult industry for

those starting out. But to succeed in any walk of life you're going to need grit, drive and determination. And you're going to need a way to overcome—and maybe even enjoy—the obstacles that will, without any doubt, be put in your way. Here are some of the ways that worked for me.

👓 *If you're going through hell, keep going*

This first one isn't original to me. I always thought it belonged to Winston Churchill, who certainly knew a thing or two about how to get himself and other people through tough times. If he never said it, he should have done.

At times in the first nine years of my acting career, I did feel like I was going through hell. And most of us do at one time or another. I kept going then out of a mixture of anger, fear, determination and necessity. There was nothing else I could do. I wanted to be an actor and I was going to go through whatever I had to go through to do it.

Even when I had achieved stardom, I could never quite believe that each film would not be my last, and there certainly were a lot that could have killed off my career and sent me back to hell if I hadn't kept going and, somehow, just at the right moment, pulled off a success—*The Italian Job* in 1969,

Get Carter and *Sleuth* in the early 1970s, *The Man Who Would Be King* in 1975, another John Huston film, *Escape to Victory*, in 1981, *Hannah and Her Sisters* in 1986. The list goes on.

In the 1990s I effectively retired. Well, I didn't retire, the movies retired me. I was in my sixties, the scripts stopped coming and I thought my acting career was over. I settled down to owning restaurants and writing my autobiography. It wasn't exactly hell, but Jack Nicholson persuaded me to keep going and, boy, was I glad I did. As it turned out, I've done some of my best work since I "retired."

⌐o *Use the difficulty*

This one I like to think is mine, although I'm happy to be told otherwise. Whenever I'm in a negative situation I tell myself to "use the difficulty": to look hard and find something positive within the problem.

Joe Levine, the president of Embassy Pictures and the guy whose photo must surely be in the picture dictionary under "American movie producer"— short, fat and with a big cigar—had put me under contract for seven years, in case I was star material, when I was cast in *Zulu*. But he was not a fan of my performance. He summoned me to his office and told me, "You know I love you, Michael..." my stomach hit the floor "...but you'll never be a romantic lead and you're not for us."

I felt dizzy. I concentrated on my breathing. "Why?" I asked, in a tear-soaked whisper.

"I know you're not, Michael," said Joe, between puffs, "but you look like a queer on screen." The 1960s was not an easy time to be gay, or to look it, and Joe released me from my contract. It was a terrible blow.

When the executives saw the rushes of *The Ipcress File* they took a similar view, sending a message to the director, Sidney Furie, that read, "Michael Caine is wearing glasses, shopping in supermarkets and cooking. He is coming across as a homosexual." That wasn't the exact message—I've cleaned it up a bit. Luckily Sid took no notice. In fact, he used the difficulty. When the girl (played by Sue Lloyd) asks if I always wear my glasses, I say, in Harry Palmer's rather low-key, anti-hero way, "I only take them off in bed." She reaches over and takes them off. It's now considered to be one of the great moments of movie seduction.

After my devastating interview with Joe Levine I used the difficulty. The BBC was filming *Hamlet at Elsinore* and Dennis, my agent, always looking for ways to enhance my reputation and extend my range, got me the part of Horatio to Christopher

Plummer's Prince. I had had no classical training and was not well acquainted with iambic pentameter but I decided that if what I was conveying on screen was ambiguous sexuality, I would go with it, rather than fighting it, and use the difficulty to bring out that aspect of Horatio's personality.

And then I got the opportunity to scotch the difficulty, playing Alfie, one of the most notorious heterosexuals ever to appear on film.

Later, I understood that having spent a large part of my life as a loser, I did not come across on screen as an obvious winner in the way that, say, Peter O'Toole or Charles Bronson did. I didn't mind: I decided that having been a loser added an interesting dimension to my personality, and decided to make it part of my appeal. I have often played losers in pictures, and you get paid just as much as you do when you're playing a winner.

Later still, I had to face up to a particularly wounding difficulty. One day when I was on the cusp of middle age I was sent a script. I happened to be in a bit of a lull but, nonetheless, when I read it I sent it straight back, appalled, saying the part wasn't big enough. Barely worth doing at all. A couple of hours later the producer was on the phone: "Michael, there's been a misunderstanding. We don't want you to play the romantic juvenile. We were thinking of you as the father." I looked in the mirror, appalled again, but for an entirely different reason, and decided to use that difficulty too. Getting older is much easier for actors than for actresses. All the best roles for an actor of my type are the mature ones, and since I accepted I was the father, not the lover, the parts have just got juicier and more interesting.

I was still using the difficulty even on my most recent film, at the age of eighty-three. *King of Thieves* is based on the true story of five old men who commit a massive bank robbery in London's diamond district over an Easter holiday weekend. The youngest of them, who was not arrested with the others, was said to be in his sixties. When, in court, the other four were asked why they had let him take all the stolen gold, one explained: "He was the only one who could carry the bag." My difficulty was that I desperately wanted to visit Brian Reader, the character I was playing, in prison, so that I could hear his voice. The police wouldn't let me, but the screen writer had interviewed Reader's daughter about the film and had told her that her father was to be played by Michael Caine. "Oh, my father, represented on screen by a British icon, how wonderful!" she did not say. What she did say, apparently, was, "Oh, Michael Caine, he's much too common." Insult piled on difficulty, but I used it. It meant I didn't have to adopt a thick Cockney accent in the movie, and everyone, even Americans, would be able to understand the dialogue.

As I'm writing I've just heard that another imprisoned member of the gang, Terry Perkins, played by Tom Courtenay in the movie, has died in his sleep. He had just been told, as they all had, that if they didn't return the money, their sentences would be increased. Terry Perkins used the difficulty. But don't try this at home.

And my latest big break—literally. Early in 2018, I was trying to settle down to writing this book but, of course, I was often distracted with other work or social occasions. Pottering about in the garden one weekend after yet another snowfall, I slipped and fell and managed to break my ankle. I was in terrible pain, and confined to bed or a wheelchair for weeks. It was in many ways hellish, especially for my wife. But I used the difficulty. Since I couldn't really go out, or do anything very much, I sat at home and got on with writing.

👓 Blessings (and curses) in disguise

Disasters are not always as bad as they first appear. Some of my biggest knockbacks turned out to be for the best.

In 1961, I did a two-week run of a play called

Why the Chicken? (no, I don't know either) written by John McGrath and directed by Lionel Bart, who had become a good friend. I was then very disappointed not to get the part of Bill Sykes when Lionel Bart went on to do *Oliver!*. It would have been a great part for me, and steady work, at a time when work was hard to come by. Two years later I took one of my worst knocks when I messed up my audition and was turned down for the part of *Alfie* in the London stage play.

I soon came to see both of these disappointments as blessings in disguise. The stage play of *Alfie* ran for three weeks in New York, and although it managed to transfer to the West End in London it was not a huge hit. The film on the other hand...well, it was a triumph. *Oliver!* was still running six years later, the day I drove past the theatre in my Rolls-Royce, fresh from my U.S. publicity tour for *Alfie* and feeling like a star. I shuddered as I drove by. That actor's name had been up there in lights since 1961: six years. I would have missed out on so much.

I was disappointed again to have to turn down Troy Kennedy Martin's offer to put me in his new TV series, *Z Cars*. Two years previously I'd have jumped at the chance, but now I was in the movies. Troy said, "OK, I'll write you a film, then." He used the difficulty. And he wrote a little film for me called *The Italian Job*.

Apparent triumphs can be deceiving too.

One of the worst pictures I ever made—and there is healthy competition for that title—was *The Swarm*. It was 1977, and since the success of *The Man Who Would Be King*, I had done my usual thing: a series of films that each fell short in various ways.

I was to play alongside a stunning cast, all brilliant actors and extremely experienced movie stars: Henry Fonda, José Ferrer, Olivia de Havilland, Richard Widmark and Fred MacMurray. The director, Irwin Allen, was a friend and had just produced *The Towering Inferno* with Steve McQueen, Paul Newman and a galaxy of other big names, earning eight Academy Awards and the highest box office of 1974. I was a young foreign actor overcome by the glamour of Hollywood. Of course I said yes.

When it was released in 1978 *The Swarm* quickly gained a reputation as the worst movie ever made. Irwin Allen was a brilliant producer but brilliant producers do not always translate into brilliant directors. The script, which I had hardly bothered to read in my excitement, was dreadful. And if I'd taken even a little time to think it over I would have seen that a burning skyscraper is high-stakes visual drama, whereas a swarm of bees is—well, it turns out it's just ridiculous. And messy. Shooting our first scenes with the bees, we noticed little black dots appearing on our clothes. The bees were shitting on us. Sadly, they weren't the only ones. When the film was released the audiences and critics did the same.

None of my co-stars seemed to care. I realised that, although they were all huge stars, they were also old stars, and I wondered: had they reached a point in their careers when they would have said yes to anything for the money.

I was disappointed. This was only my second Hollywood film. I'd made other movies but none in Hollywood itself. But I used the difficulty. Whenever I was not in a scene, instead of going to my dressing room I sat on set for hours, watching these Hollywood legends and absorbing as much as I could. One of the techniques I learnt on that movie was the power of stillness. These actors did not fidget around all the time. They kept very still, and their gestures, when they made them, were clean and deliberate. I also noticed how calm and relaxed they kept themselves, and how unafraid they were of trying things and making mistakes.

Richard Widmark wanted to impart to me one very specific piece of advice, which I now, in the spirit of paying it forward, pass along to you. I was on set with Richard and Henry Fonda. We were waiting around for our scene and Richard said to me, "Take care around the special effects, Michael, especially in the cowboy movies."

"Why, Dick?" I asked. I didn't really understand what he meant.

"What?" he replied. "Could you stand on the other side of me and say that again?"

"Why is that, Dick?" I said, louder, into his other ear.

He said, "You know when the cowboy looks out from behind a rock and a bullet pings past him and he ducks back and then there's a great big rock explosion? Well, now that cowboy is deaf in one ear."

"What's that he's saying?" said Henry, squinting and cupping his ear with his hand.

"You did a lot of Westerns, too, didn't you, Hank?" I shouted into the cupped ear.

"Yeah, I did," said Henry.

You would have thought I would also have learnt never to pick a film with stars in my eyes. But sadly I made that mistake several more times. Just a year later I was offered a part in an action adventure movie set in Kenya called *Ashanti*. My co-stars were to be William Holden, Rex Harrison, Omar Sharif and Peter Ustinov. What could go wrong? Everything. The director left. The female lead left. The script was rewritten. We were all contractually obliged to finish the picture and we did. Never heard of it? Good.

In 1990 I made a movie called *Bullseye* with my great friend Michael Winner directing and my great friend Roger Moore co-starring. We had a lot of fun making it but nobody had any fun watching it, if indeed anybody actually did. *Bullseye* turned out to be the most inappropriate title for a film ever. We didn't even hit the target.

I grew up in England, where the autumn is cold and rainy and the winter is colder and rainier. And then I lived for a number of years in Los Angeles, where every day of the year the sun shines and it's 80 degrees Fahrenheit. Now, I love Los Angeles. I was very happy living there and I still have a lot of good friends there. But I prefer England. In the end, I missed the seasons. Here, we see the first daffodil of spring and we appreciate it. We think, We've earned that. We think, Isn't God good, giving us the spring again?

Bad things happen to all of us at some point in our lives. We lose our jobs, or our parents, or our health. We are disappointed at work, or in love, or in front of the mirror. You can choose to dwell on the knockbacks. Or you can choose to embrace the opportunities that are still available to you.

Someone once asked me the secret of my success and my answer was "survival." I'm still here. I'm still going, even if sometimes I'm going through hell. In the end, success is survival.

4.

Doing the Right Things

"It's not who you are under-neath. It's what you do that defines you."

Batman Begins, 2005

IF YOU MAKE IT in your universe, it's because you keep doing enough of the right things. It sounds simple. It *is* simple, really.

👓 *Just say yes*

I can't think of a single example of an opportunity that, taking everything into account, I have regretted taking. I don't like to look back with regret: what's the point? And I can always find something good for me even in bad situations. If the script was terrible, maybe the location was fun. If the location was a steaming jungle or a frozen wasteland, maybe the director was a genius. If the director was dialling it in, maybe my co-stars made it interesting. If all else fails, I can always learn from whatever mistake got me there in the first place.

I also can't think of a single example of an opportunity I turned down, then wished I hadn't. That's for different reasons. That's mainly because my approach has always been to grasp every bloody opportunity that appears in front of me. So, it's hard to remember any opportunity I turned down, and if I did, it was to take a different one. And I never regret taking opportunities. QED.

Success comes from doing. The best way to keep doing enough of the right things is to keep doing a lot of things. Even if some of those things end up being flops, you'll be building up your experience, building relationships, building confidence, opening up opportunities, keeping life fresh and learning your craft. So long as enough of them are good enough, you will be allowed to keep going.

When I was struggling to get work, saying yes to anything that came along was the obvious thing to do. I didn't just need the experience, I needed the money. The offers were so thin on the ground that I had to go one further than saying yes. Most of the time, there was nothing on offer to me at all, so it was up to me to go out and make someone say yes to me.

That's how I came to get a part in Johnny Speight's 1961 tense TV two-hander *The Compartment*, set in a railway carriage. Somehow I happened to be in the producer John McGrath's office (he of *Why the Chicken?*) and John mentioned a script on his desk that was going to be his next TV show.

He left the room, for some reason, and I picked it up. There was a part in it that was perfect for me (really the only part—it was a two-hander but essentially it was a forty-five-minute monologue): a vulgar Cockney, who eventually goes mad with frustration at his travelling companion's snobbish refusal to talk to him, and kills him. It was a bigger, more difficult part than I had ever played on television but it wasn't going to be a stretch for me to work myself up into a frenzy about a posh git, and I begged John to give me the part. And he did.

The Compartment was my first chance to demonstrate that I could carry a show, and it brought me to the attention of all sorts of important people, including Dennis Selinger, who agreed to become my agent and steered me towards *Next Time I'll Sing To You* and ever onwards; Troy Kennedy Martin, who later wrote *The Italian Job*; Bill Naughton, who later wrote *Alfie*; and Roger Moore, who was to become one of my closest friends. It was another of those little breaks that added up to the big breaks. Another of those little steps on the staircase, those little pieces in the jigsaw puzzle.

But even after *Alfie* had propelled me into a different world—one in which I never had to do an audition or a screen test, or beg for a role again—I couldn't shake the idea that every movie was my last. I never felt confident that the good times would last. So I just kept on saying yes, kept on doing. Even though I never had a contract with a movie studio that wasn't torn up after my first movie, I conducted my whole career as if I was on a 1930s-style Hollywood contract: I did as many films each year as I could. Between *Alfie* in 1966 and *The Italian Job* in 1969, I did *Gambit*, playing a con-man opposite Shirley MacLaine; *Funeral in Berlin*, a second Harry Palmer picture; *Hurry Sundown*, where I premiered my Deep South accent opposite Jane Fonda; *Tonite Let's All Make Love in London*, a documentary about London's pop culture directed by Peter Whitehead, who invented the music video, and featuring Edna O'Brien, Vanessa Redgrave, Julie Christie, David Hockney and Mick Jagger; *Billion Dollar Brain*, a third Harry Palmer set in Finland and, I think, a really atmospheric and underrated picture; *Woman Times Seven* with Shirley MacLaine again; *The Magus*, about which the less said the better, and that's easy because I still have no idea what it was about; *Deadfall*, written and directed by my old friend Bryan Forbes, in which I played a jewel thief; and *Play Dirty*, a war film initially to have been directed by René Clément but taken over by André De Toth.

And, yes, my approach did mean that, over the course of my career, I made a lot of bad movies—

because I made a lot of movies. But for the same reason—because I made a lot of movies—I also made a lot of good movies. On the TV shows where they selected the year's best and worst films I was usually on both lists. Did I regret the bad ones? Well, it didn't feel good when the critics ripped into me, but they paid just as well as the good ones. The point is, there is no sure-fire way to tell in advance which ones are going to flop. So the best way to do a lot of good work is to do a lot of work. Don't overthink it. Don't agonise. Just go ahead and do it, and enjoy it, and learn from it.

Success comes from doing. Don't wait for your chances: go out and take them. Don't spend your life sitting off to the side, waiting for the perfect part in the perfect script with the perfect director at the perfect fee. Don't wait passively, patiently for the perfect project to deliver itself to you wrapped in a bow. Or even the perfect man or woman. Say yes, and make this one the one you've been dreaming of. Learn the confidence you can only gain through experience. Achieve the relaxation you can only gain through confidence. Give the performance you can only give when you're relaxed enough to access all your resources.

👓 *Whatever it is, give it 100 per cent*

On your way up, that might mean spending time on things you think are below you. Taking work that you think is below you. Watching others—maybe your contemporaries, maybe your friends—becoming successful while you are still on the bottom rung. Watching others settling into married bliss while you are still kissing frogs. Keep doing it anyway. If you sit around waiting for the big part, then how are you going to be ready for it when it finally comes along? It's the small-time experience that adds up to the big-time ability.

My advice to any actor is, your part may not be the most important part in the movie, but it is the most important thing to you. Your contribution is what you can control so, however big or small it is, you have to make it as good as it can be. That doesn't mean doing silly things to attract attention. Don't twitch away or neurotically worry at insignificant details or constantly try to catch the director's eye. All of that is just annoying and makes you look needy. Just make it real, make it true and make bloody sure you know your lines. Treat your small part as if it's the main event—because, for you, it is. Approach the small part you're playing right now as the most important thing there is right now. Give it everything you've got.

The same goes whatever you're doing, in whatever walk of life. However scaled down your role is, do not make that a reason to scale down your effort. If the part falls short of what you wanted, don't let that be a reason for you to fall short of what the director wants. You are not making it up to yourself: you are doing yourself down.

In fact, in some ways, small parts are more difficult, so you have to work even harder to pull them off. You have one thing to do, all eyes are on you when you mess it up, and if you don't have a second line you don't get a second chance. So don't think you can multi-task. Don't use the time you will inevitably be hanging around to clear emails, take a nap or catch up on the news. Go through your lines (or line). Go through them (or it) again. And again. Think about your character. Stay alert to what's going on around you and what you can learn from it. Stay in the moment of *this* role, *this* task. If you're in the right business for you, it will be more fun than Candy Crush, and it will pay better too.

These days, I love small parts. They can be much more interesting and I don't have to get up at six thirty in the morning to learn pages of dialogue. My motto at this stage in my career is: "It doesn't matter how small it is, so long as it's deep." But no matter the size of the part, I would never get caught giving less than 100 per cent. Why do anything if you're not going to do it as well as you possibly can?

🕶 *Learn your craft*

I can't emphasise this strongly enough. You have to learn your craft. Whatever it is you want to do, you have to put in the hours to learn everything you're going to need, starting with the basics. Because if you're confident in your craft—be it cooking, plumbing, selling, whatever—then when the next challenge comes along, you'll feel able to say yes, and you'll be able to give yourself to it, 100 per cent.

How do you learn? There is no single way. Learn from classes, if you can, but don't worry if you can't. I would have loved to spend three years studying voice and movement and the classical repertoire at RADA, but that option wasn't open to me. And, anyway, the alternative course I accidentally took instead, with no choice in the matter, is one I would highly recommend.

I didn't go to drama school so most of my learning was on-the-job or on-the-bus. On the bus and the Tube, I learnt voice and movement and character, from watching how people behaved. On the job, I learnt lessons of technique that I used throughout my career and still draw on every day

I am on set; I built skills and confidence that prepared me for anything and everything the business
could throw at me. My years in draughty repertory
theatres, my brief unsuccessful stint in Joan Littlewood's Theatre Workshop and my endless bit parts
on TV and one-line movie roles formed my appren-
ticeship, and for an actor I still think there can be
no better start.

In repertory in Horsham, Alwyn D. Fox taught
me, at my very first rehearsal, to project my voice
to the back of the auditorium: "The person sitting
at the back has paid as much as anyone else to hear
every word you have to say." After I had accepted a
pick 'n' mix sweet from a member of the audience
during a bit where no one on stage was speaking
to me, he screamed me an explanation about the
"fourth wall" and its role in sustaining the illusion
of theatre. "How dare you break it? The fourth wall
is the invisible wall between us and the audience,
and if you break it the magic of theatre is completely destroyed."

I learnt a range of accents, from Chicago gangster
to Lord of the Manor via Ireland, Scotland, Wales
and the north country, which came in very handy
years later when Cy Endfield was considering me for
the role of the army officer in *Zulu*. I learnt how
to time a funny line. I suffered from terrible stage
fright and used to keep a bucket in the wings into

which I would throw up most evenings until, grad-ually, I learnt how to be relaxed on stage.

In repertory in Lowestoft my director also gave me an early lesson in how to create an impact by do-ing less: how to be, rather than perform. This was excellent advice for a theatre actor and, as I realised years later, crucial advice for a film actor.

I was cast as a drunkard, and at my first rehearsal I came staggering onto the stage, then swayed about a bit. The director held up his hand.

"Stop. What are you doing, Michael?"

"I'm drunk in this scene," I explained, failing to hide my irritation that it had not been apparent.

"I know that," he said. "But what are you doing? You're giving me an actor *playing* a drunk. I'm pay-ing you to *be* a drunk. You're trying to talk slurred and walk crooked. A real drunk is trying to speak clearly and walk straight."

My wise and wily repertory theatre director had summed up movie acting in one line, and I remem-ber it and use it to this day.

My repertory theatre training came into its own any time I had to remember a lot of lines, or do something truly terrifying. In rep, you do fifty dif-ferent plays a year. You have to remember two hours of dialogue every night, and rehearse a different two hours of dialogue for next week's play during the day.

That grounding gave me the confidence to beg John McGrath to give me the part in *The Compartment*—a forty-five-minute monologue, delivered live—and the experience to pull it off. (Although I can't prove this to you: a few years later I asked the BBC for a copy of the tape and they wrote back to say they had been on an economy drive and had recorded something else over it. So my first serious piece of TV work was gone for ever. I wondered whether they had also recorded over Laurence Olivier and John Gielgud. I decided not to go mad with frustration and kill anybody but I was a bit disappointed.)

It came in handy again in 1964 when I was given another big opportunity, starring in the TV play *The Other Man*, about what might have happened if Britain had surrendered to Germany in 1940. At two hours long, *The Other Man* was ITV's longest ever TV play. There was a cast of two hundred, sixty of whom had speaking parts, a twenty-minute stop for the news and several commercial breaks. And, yes, again, to top it all off, the play was broadcast live.

The exposure was high-stakes and the circumstances could hardly have been tougher but my co-star Siân Phillips was a wonderful actress, which helped, and I swear I didn't forget one line. (A couple of people did, but fortunately for them we had a high-tech solution in the form of a lady with a button on a wire and a script, who followed whoever was speaking around the set. If someone dried up, she would push the button, sound transmission would be cut and she would read the actor the line. I imagined people all over Britain banging their silent TVs and cursing in unison.)

Repertory theatre and the training it offered young actors no longer exists in anything like the same form. Now it's the pre-recorded TV shows that provide work and experience for young actors, but they can't possibly provide the adrenalin-fuelled tightrope-walk training of live performing. Or the vocal training, which is probably the reason I can't hear or understand a lot of the dialogue on TV, these days.

A short stint at Joan Littlewood's legendary Theatre Workshop in the mid-fifties was the closest I ever came to drama school. Joan was a brilliant woman whose Communist theatre company followed the "method" acting principles of Russian actor and director Konstantin Stanislavski long before they became popular in the West, and the political principles of Vladimir Lenin when they were all the rage in certain parts of London. Despite being a genuine member of the proletariat, I struggled to fit in there. One of the Theatre Workshop's principles was the sublimation of the individual to the ensemble and, though I did try to sublimate myself, Joan made it clear from the outset that she was not impressed. "Stop," she said, the moment I stepped on stage for the first rehearsal. "What are you doing?"

"I'm rehearsing," I said, mystified as to why she had stopped me.

"This is a group theatre, Michael," she said. "Get off. Come on again."

So I went off, and came on again, trying harder to be ensemble-y.

"No," shouted Joan, immediately I reappeared from the wings. "I'm not having it."

"Having what?" I asked. Joan was the first Communist I had met since my time in the army in Korea and I had to remind myself that this Communist I was not supposed to kill.

"All of this star business, Michael. It won't do."

As soon as the show was over, she fired me. "Piss off to the West End," she said. "You will never be an actor. You will only ever be a star."

It wasn't hard to find the blessing inside that particular disguise. Someone had called me a star, even if that someone thought "star" was a dirty capitalist word.

Also, even in the short time I spent in her company before she threw me out, Joan taught me two very important lessons in "method" acting that remained a part of my craft. She taught me the "sense memory" technique that takes you back to your own real-life experiences to help you access emotion when you need it. And she told me: "The rehearsal is the work, the performance is the relaxation." Meaning that, by the time you get to the performance, you should be so familiar with what you're doing that it seems effortless. (More on that in Chapter Six.) Joan made an incredible contribution to British working-class theatre, for which I salute her. I am also eternally grateful to her for the contribution she made to my own professional education.

Unfortunately, when I started to make the move from theatre to film acting, it became clear that I had to start my education almost from scratch. I had to retrain my voice, which was like a foghorn from years of bellowing up to the back of the balcony. Remembering lines in the movies was a whole other business from remembering them on stage or even on TV. There was no time for the kinds of actor-focused rehearsals I was used to: a gentle read-through, discussions of motivation and relationships, maybe a little improvisation, trying a scene this way and that. The time was instead spent on technical considerations and the coordination of confusing film equipment, all of which served only to tauten my jangling nerves to screaming point.

In my first movie *A Hill in Korea* in 1956, I had eight lines, which I had to deliver at the rate of one line a week. Each week, by the time the first assistant had shouted, "Quiet," then "Turnover," and the camera technicians had turned on their machines and the sound man had called, "Speed," and the assistant had yelled, "Mark it," and the clapper boy had run in with the clapperboard and brought it down with a bang and rushed out of shot, and the director, Julian Amyes, had shouted "Action!," I had worked myself into a state of such abject terror at the thought of forgetting my one line that I would, indeed, completely forget my one line. At which point the director shouted, "Cut," and the assistant called, "We're going again, don't break it up," and the director said to the continuity girl, as everyone tried with varying degrees of effort and success to hide their disgust, "Give him the line." The assistant shouted, "Going again," and the whole process started again. Even when I did finally manage to remember the line, I was terrible.

𝄇 *Be prepared to fail*

I could have gone back to the theatre, where at least I didn't feel like a rank amateur any more. Instead I said yes to dozens more one-line movie parts, and gradually I got better.

In *The Day the Earth Caught Fire*, a classic British apocalypse movie released in 1961, Eddie Judd played the lead role and I played a policeman. I had to hold up the traffic, direct the cars one way and the trucks the other, then say my one line. It was a complicated piece of business that would surely have floored me in my early movie-acting days, but by now I was more experienced and finally I nailed it.

"Quiet."

"Turnover."

"Speed."

"Mark it."

"Action."

Cameras rolled, cars and trucks rolled and my policeman's helmet rolled down over my eyes and apparently over my brain too. I couldn't see the cars and trucks, and I couldn't remember my line.

The lesson is not about hats. (Or not only about hats. Note to all: don't let hats distract you from your goals.) It is about the value of experience, even (or especially) the most humiliating experience. *The Day the Earth Caught Fire* was mortifying. The director actually said to me words that I thought were just a cliché: "You'll never work in this industry again." Well, I did work in movies again a few times after that, but I never again allowed a hat to distract me.

And, after *Zulu*, I never allowed shirt buttons to

ruin a take. In one dramatic scene I was required to climb up and then jump off a burning roof, while ranks of Zulus came closer and closer. It was a big set piece involving the stunts team, lots of special fire safety procedures and hundreds of extras. The fire had to burn in just the right way. The wind had to be blowing in the right direction. It took a long time to get the shot set up. When we finally finished the scene the continuity girl said, "Oh, wait. Michael's shirt was buttoned all the way up in the earlier sequence, and now he has two buttons undone." Silly bugger, I had undone them between takes without thinking about it, I expect because of the intense heat. We had to set up from scratch and shoot it all again.

I learnt the lessons by making the mistakes—but I only made each one once.

👓 *Never stop learning*

Once I had left school I loved learning. With just one or two exceptions. Whatever your line of work, there will be some skills you have to acquire that give you very little pleasure.

For me, it was horses. My daughter Dominique turned out to be a magnificent horsewoman but she must have got it from her mother, or my father, who was in the Royal Horse Artillery in the war. My first shot in *Zulu* required me to ride a horse, something I had confidently told Cy End-field I could do. I had, it was true, taken lessons in Wimbledon. The first lesson ended when I fell off in front of a bus. The second lesson ended when I fell off in front of a bicycle. There was no third lesson. The horse I was assigned to ride in my first shot in *Zulu* seemed as unhappy with the situation as I was. Long story short, he wouldn't move at all, then he reared up, like something out of the Spanish Riding School, and bolted towards a cliff edge. By this time we were losing the light. So my first appearance in my first ever major motion picture is not me but the prop man, Ginger, wear-ing my hat and cape. The following day the horse and I were reunited, and he took the opportunity to cement our relationship by throwing me into a pond.

Later I had to learn to scuba dive for *Beyond the Poseidon Adventure*, which was an even greater chal-lenge. I hadn't learnt to swim until I was twelve, and the last time I had worn equipment like that, it had been as a six-year-old soon-to-be-evacuated child, testing out a gas mask during the Second World War. Mine was faulty: when I ran around with it on, as instructed, I promptly passed out. I was assured that the technology had improved since then. Nonetheless a professional diver was posted close by to whisk me to the surface if I raised my hand.

And for *Battle of Britain* I was required to squeeze myself into the cockpit of a Spitfire, and speed along as if about to take off. At the time I couldn't drive a car, let alone fly. As we were setting up the shot, Ginger Lacey, the Battle of Britain veteran who was coaching me, yelled, "Whatever you do, don't touch the red button."

The red button? I looked down and, sure enough, there by my left knee was a big red button. "Why not?" I bawled back over the noise of the engine turning over.

"You'll take off," he shouted breezily.

"Action!" yelled the director. In a state of abject terror I shifted over to the right as far as I could and hurtled off, the only squadron leader ever to prepare for takeoff with his legs crossed.

But apart from the horses, and the diving, and the flying—basically, I like to keep my feet on the ground—I was always happy to learn. In whatever line of work, technology changes, tastes change, the business model changes. I still learn something new on every project. A few years ago I made my first 3D film, *Journey 2: The Mysterious Island*, based on the Jules Verne story. We filmed on location in Hawaii but there was also a lot of acting in front of green screens and in light theatres, which involves standing surrounded by six thousand lights in front of eight cameras and moving into every conceivable position. After that they can manipulate your image in various ways without you being there. In 2014 I made a film called *Youth* in which I played a retired composer, with a great cast including Harvey Keitel, Rachel Weisz, Paul Dano and my old friend from our 1967 movie, *Hurry Sundown*, Jane Fonda. The director, Paolo Sorrentino, introduced me to a new way of working that had been made possible by a change in the technology. Because everything was now digital and computerised, there was no need to stop work to change the film in the camera every ten minutes or so. At first that seemed like a big disadvantage for the actors learning their lines, because Paolo Sorrentino liked to do tremendously long takes that just kept going and going, and eventually someone was going to fluff a line or make a mistake. But the upside was, when one of us did dry, we didn't have to cut and go all the way back to the beginning of the scene, as we always used to, then start again. We could just go back a couple of lines. Plus, I learnt how to conduct an orchestra. What a wonderful feeling!

So I'm always learning my craft. I learnt from classes, from reading, from listening, from watching, from stealing (but only from the best). But most of all I learnt, and continue to learn, from doing. I do it; I make mistakes; I learn from my mistakes. Nothing has the power to etch a lesson deeper into my brain than making a mistake. Nothing builds resilience better than making a mistake and then getting up and trying again, and doing it a bit better.

You may not see the results straight away but everything you're doing counts. So keep doing it. And if you keep doing the right things for long enough, eventually the stars align.

PART TWO

Making the Cut

5.

Getting There Is Just the Start

Harry: "Clever sod, aren't you?"
Jack: "Only comparatively."

Get Carter, 1973

THERE WAS A MOMENT, and I can remember that moment exactly, when I felt like it was happening and I was making it. I was in New York for the first time, doing my first ever American publicity tour, for *Alfie*. My room in the Plaza Hotel had a view over Central Park, and New York looked just like it did in the movies. Outside the NBC studio at the Rockefeller Center, I was mobbed by fans wanting autographs. But *I* was wide-eyed and starstruck too: at a restaurant called Elaine's, which was soon to become a firm favourite, I knocked over Woody Allen's wine glass and trod on Ursula Andress's foot. *Alfie* was my first movie to go on general release in the United States—an almost unheard-of event at that time for a small British picture. But the moment I felt it was happening for me came when I was standing outside the back of Bloomingdale's on Lexington Avenue and looked across the street to see a movie theatre playing *The Ipcress File*. *Alfie* was doing so well that Universal had bought *The Ipcress File* and, even though it was

now eighteen months old, put that on general release too. Now I had two films on general release in
the U.S., and an Oscar nomination for *Alfie* to boot.

I felt like I was making it, but I didn't feel like
I'd made it. I never relaxed, never assumed the good
times would roll on for ever, never let my guard
down. I knew that I had to keep nailing it, keep
not mucking it up, keep going to work and delivering the goods and doing a good job every day. Even
when you're making it, you have to keep on making
it, day after day.

👓 *Turning up, body and mind*

This was where the discipline from the army, and
my years of experience in repertory and doing bit
parts, came into its own. After *Alfie* was released in
1966, I made twelve movies in four years. It was
the sixties, but there was no "Turn on, tune in, drop
out" for me. For me, it was "Turn up, don't muck
it up, get on."

Before you even get to your performance, before
the cameras start to roll, before the work starts, you
have to turn up—on time, alert and ready for whatever mental and physical challenges the day is going
to bring. I'm talking about the absolute basics of
professionalism and courtesy here. So many people

fail to pay these things enough attention, yet just by taking care of the basics you can put yourself well ahead of the game. None of this is glamorous. It's a lot like getting ready for school. But then film-making—and I'm assured the same goes in the supposedly glamorous worlds of modelling, fashion design, PR and air travel—is not glamorous: it's just a lot of hard work.

So, these are my basics for making sure I turn up ready to perform. I learnt them as a young actor but I still stick by them today. Number one: I always have my magic travel bag packed and by the door before I go to bed. Whether I'm going on location for three months, or popping into the set for half a day, I think through what I need to take with me, not in the morning in a mild panic but calmly the night before.

Number two: I have to get a good night's sleep and, even more importantly, I have to have a fail-safe plan to be sure I'm up in time in the morning: one alarm clock good, two alarm clocks better.

Three: I make sure I know how I'm going to get to the studio or location or wherever I need to be, and how long it will take me to get there. I build in extra time for unexpected traffic, or the bus being late, or finding a parking spot. If someone else has made transport arrangements for me, is that person going to be available at the end of a phone at whatever unpleasant time of the morning I have to leave, in case the arrangements don't go to plan? A lot can go wrong with transport, and if you don't know how you're getting there, you may not have a job when you eventually appear, late and flustered, looking disorganised. I always mentally rehearse each step of the journey, anticipate the problems and have a back-up plan.

A calm, unrushed journey to work is a good time to take a few deep breaths and give myself a pep talk. I skip the pep talk, these days, but it used to be something along the lines of: "You've come this far. You don't want to go back where you came from." That gave me the motivation to get through whatever I had to get through.

By the time I turned up for my first day of rehearsals on *Sleuth* in 1972, I had played major roles in around twenty pictures. I had been around the block a few times. But I was very nervous because this was a two-hander and the other hand was going to be Laurence Olivier—or, to give him his proper title, Lord Olivier—the founder of the country's brand new National Theatre and at that time the most celebrated actor in the world. As I sat in the car on the way to Pinewood Studios, I gave myself a talking-to: "Larry Olivier might be a giant of the stage and screen, one of the greatest actors of all time, and, yes, I might be only the greatest actor from the Elephant and Castle, but I'm good at what I do. So I'm just going to do what I do, and not allow myself to be intimidated by him or his reputation. I'm going to give him a run for his money." (I was still very nervous when I got there. And I remained ill-at-ease even when the great man arrived at ten on the dot and made straight for me, hand outstretched, eyes twinkling. "Michael," he boomed, "we meet at last." He could not have been friendlier or more welcoming to me, but I felt acutely conscious that what I was dealing with here was a quite formidable force. The pep talk helped a bit.)

Pep talk over, deep breaths taken, I have now arrived on time and in the right frame of mind. It's a good start.

Now I get my bearings. I establish where I need to go and what I need to do.

In movie-making that will mean finding my dressing room, Makeup and Hair, locating exactly where we are going to be shooting, then getting myself into makeup, hair and costume. In most other lines of work, you will have put on your "costume"—maybe a uniform, or maybe that outfit that makes you look good and feel quietly confident—before you left the house.

I find the people I'm going to be working with and introduce myself. On a movie set, I always make a particular point of seeing the assistant director, whose job it is to call the actors to the set when it's their moment. If you aren't on a movie set, there will often be someone with a clipboard who is coordinating the logistics. Make yourself known to them.

If you are going to be using any kit or technical equipment, track it down and test it. If you are conducting an interview, check the batteries on your voice recorder. If you are giving a presentation, review your slides on the laptop, check the mike, stand at the lectern.

For me, this is the time to check out the set before it fills with technicians. If it's supposed to be my home or office, I'll look like an idiot if I don't know which way the door opens, or whether it leads to the bathroom or into a cupboard. Even a moment's hesitation will destroy the illusion. It all needs to be natural and automatic, as it is in my real home or office. I pick up the props I'm going to be using too. I check they work and note where they're going to be placed. Unless I'm trying to show that my character is absent-minded or distracted, I should know exactly where I put down my glass or where I hung up my bag and how to switch on the bedside light.

If the set is supposed to be somewhere I have never been before, that's different. On *Sleuth*, my character was going to be entering the set as a stranger. I didn't want to go blundering about but I didn't want to over-familiarise myself with it either. The camera sees lack of spontaneity just as keenly as it sees hesitation. So I took myself off and walked things through quietly, once.

One last bit of kit. I always have a pencil on me so I can take notes on the moves. ("The first thing you need to become an actor is a pencil!" Alwyn D. Fox of Horsham Repertory Theatre screamed at me on my first day. Alwyn D. Fox did scream a lot, but he was usually right.)

Now I have to keep myself pristine and maintain my energy levels. I must not smear mayonnaise all over my makeup. I have to avoid that chair, where someone has abandoned half a slice of Victoria sponge. My costume and I probably shouldn't go for a little wander in the rain. And I have to eat as sensibly as I can. I won't necessarily be able to eat when I'm hungry—we may have to keep shooting—so I have to know myself well enough to grab something before I start to keel over.

Taking care of these basic requirements gives me confidence in myself. Confidence allows me to relax, and relaxation allows me to perform. Nailing the basics also makes me appear reliable, which is how you make sure they ask you to come back.

👓 *Depend on it*

Reliability is at a premium in the movies and, I'm ready to bet, everywhere else. Time is money, and holding things up because you haven't planned properly, or haven't worked out what is expected of you, or for any other reason within your control, is a drain on the producer's money and your reputation.

But it's not just turning up on time, and keeping the butter off your chin and your shoes shiny. It's also about functioning well under pressure, when the camera rolls, about bobbing back up no matter what gets flung at you, whether it's your hat coming down over your eyes or your director setting fire to your script. It's about anticipating and avoiding whatever gets you flustered or distracted, anticipating and avoiding hunger and exhaustion. It's about maintaining a high level of alert competence, even when there appears to be chaos all around you. That comes from focus and experience.

I wanted to make reliability part of my personal brand. I wanted people to say, "If you get Michael Caine, you're going to have a laugh on set, but you're getting a professional. You're getting someone who always knows his lines, who always hits his mark and who's always doing the best job he can possibly do." I wanted people, when they had worked with me once, to want to work with me again.

And, if you look at the directors I've worked with, I think I succeeded. I worked with several great ones more than once, starting with Julian Amyes, who gave me my first speaking roles in film (*A Hill in Korea*) and TV (*The Lark*, by Jean Anouilh), and Lewis Gilbert, who directed *Alfie* and *Educating Rita*, but who I had obviously impressed with my performance as "Thirsty Prisoner on Train" in *Carve Her Name with Pride* in 1958, right through to Christopher Nolan, who has cast me in each of the seven films he has made since I first appeared as Alfred Pennyworth in *Batman Begins* in 2005.

Because I got a reputation as a safe pair of hands I was also brought in once or twice to replace a leading man who, for whatever reason—alcohol, drugs or personal problems—couldn't make it through the movie.

Only a handful of people can get away with being unreliable.

The 1959 movie *Some Like It Hot*, one of the funniest and most daring comedies I have ever seen, starred Marilyn Monroe and was directed and produced by Billy Wilder. I never met Marilyn despite my best efforts (I must have had a bit part in a movie at Pinewood Studios when Laurence Olivier was directing Marilyn in *The Prince and the Showgirl* on the next set, each of them completely infuriating the other. I kept going over to their set but Marilyn was always with her coach, Paula Strasberg, and eventually the third assistant director Colin Clark threw me off the set. When I saw Colin portrayed by Eddie Redmayne in the 2011 film *My Week with Marilyn* I understood a little better why.) But I became close friends with Billy. One night over dinner I asked him if Marilyn Monroe had been difficult to work with. "Yes," said Billy. "She was always late and she didn't know her lines. But then," he said, after a pause, "I could have cast my Aunt Martha, and she would have been on time and she would have known her lines, but who the hell would have gone to see her?"

When I worked with Elizabeth Taylor on *Zee and Company*, written by my friend Edna O'Brien (Elizabeth played my wife, and the two of us ended up in a love triangle with Susannah York: the movie was a little ahead of its time when it was released in 1972 and did not do as well as it should have done), Elizabeth never turned up until ten o'clock in the morning. She had had it written into her contract, while the rest of us had to be in costume and makeup and ready to work by eight thirty. I used to have to do close-ups and back-of-the-head shots with the continuity girl every morning for ninety minutes until Elizabeth showed up. Then there would be a tea break—or, more accurately, a Bloody Mary break—at half past ten.

But actually, once she had arrived each day, Elizabeth was charming, no trouble at all and very professional. She never, ever messed up a line. And she could take a joke against herself too. One day when there was a lull in shooting the director Brian Hutton—the funniest director and possibly the funniest person I have ever met—told her he had been talking to some older technicians at MGM Studios in Hollywood; they had said that of all the child stars at the studio from the old days—Mickey Rooney, Margaret O'Brien and so on—she had been the only one who had not been a pain in the arse. Elizabeth inclined her head regally to receive the compliment. "Why, thank you, Brian," she purred charmingly.

After a short pause Brian went on, "So what I've been trying to figure out is, when did you become one?" We all held our breath until Elizabeth roared with laughter.

Marilyn could get away with it and so could Elizabeth. For everyone else, if you're flaky or temperamental, you have about three movies before you'll be replaced with someone who can do whatever you do, but without all the hassle. On a movie set, the continuity person writes down everything that hap-

pens, including the reason for any delay on a take—
for example, "a dog barked" or "the ceiling fell
down." Or "actor, Flaky McDitzy, one hour late."
If a movie's budget is blown, the continuity sheets
will tell the story of how and why. And if your
name is bigger on the sheets than it is at the box
office, you become unemployable. It's very clear-cut
in the movie business. But in most other industries,
word of mouth will usually do the job of continuity
sheets.

Talent will get you only so far. You need to add
in boring old reliability if you want to endure. Your
life can be disorganised, but your work can never
be. I am a disorganised person in every other aspect
of my life: I can never find my glasses or my hat,
and whenever we're going out I forget where we're
going. But I am very organised when it comes to
my work, whether on or off the set. It's professional;
it's courteous; it will get you asked again. Unless
you're confident you're as big a star in your universe
as Marilyn or Elizabeth were in theirs, I would suggest you turn up on time with a clear head, a clean
face and a pencil in your hand.

6.

The Rehearsal Is the Work

*"It's fear dries the mouth,
isn't it?"*

Zulu, 1963

THE MAIN LESSON I learnt from Joan Littlewood—the only person who ever fired me—was this: the rehearsal is the work, the performance is the relaxation. Once I had worked out what it meant—that by the time you get to the performance, you should be so familiar with what you are doing that it seems effortless—I understood its importance, in acting and in life.

This goes beyond getting the basics right—turning up on time, maintaining energy levels, checking the kit. It's about knowing your role inside out. If you can prepare thoroughly, if you can put in the spadework before the performance—or any big challenge—then you'll be more in control. You'll be more in control of your material, your nerves and yourself. That control should free you up to listen, pay attention to what is going on around you and react to whatever gets thrown at you. You have already done the work in rehearsal, you have already been through all the sweat, had all the nightmares, and when it comes to the performance you can relax, give it your best and deal with everything—from a slight change of plan to a complete and utter balls-up—from a place of alert but calm confidence.

If you do it right, preparation is not in any way opposed to spontaneity. It actually allows you to be spontaneous. When you are prepared, you are able to subdue your fear, control your nerves, channel your energy and enter that state of highly alert relaxation that is spontaneity's best friend.

In the theatre and in the movies, preparation means researching your character, working out gestures, movement and mannerisms and above all learning your lines. In the theatre you can add another layer of rehearsal with the cast. In the movies you don't get that luxury: the director will expect you to bring a fully formed characterisation with you. I reckon that Stanislavski's principle applies way beyond acting in the theatre or the movies, though. I use it when I'm cooking. I use it when I'm doing publicity interviews. As far as I can see, it's useful everywhere. Prepare the basics as thoroughly as you possibly can. Do your homework. Know your stuff. Be clear on what you have to say. So that when it comes to the moment to "perform," you're so confident in your own role that you can put your energy into listening and reacting to what is happening in the moment.

👓 *Do your research*

I always research my performances by finding and observing people who are in some respect like the part I'm going to play.

If I'm playing a real person I read about them, watch documentaries about them, find out as much as I can about them. Not so that I can do an impersonation but so that I can get a sense of their real selves, connect to their truth. My part in *Zulu* was based on a real person and, in a history book from a second-hand bookshop on the Charing Cross Road, I found a photograph of him. Lieutenant Gonville Bromhead was five foot six inches tall with a black beard and rather expressive dark eyes. The man staring out at me from the page made me want to play the part not as the chinless wonder that Cy Endfield and Stanley Baker were envisaging but as a man who, though he was ultimately overpowered, set out believing himself to be strong.

The other real people I have played on film are F. W. de Klerk, South Africa's last president under the apartheid system, in the 1997 TV film *Mandela and de Klerk* (my good friend Sidney Poitier played Nelson Mandela); Brian Reader in *King of Thieves* and—wait for it—Joseph Stalin, the murderous Soviet leader, in the 1994 TV miniseries *Then There Were Giants*. The drama focused on the three great Allied

leaders and their personal relationships with each
other during the Second World War. John Lithgow
was Roosevelt and Bob Hoskins was Churchill, and
although I was nominated for an Emmy for the role,
Bob and I got slammed by the critics as having been
miscast. At the time I think I probably agreed. The
character and the Russian accent were a stretch for
me, and because I didn't look anything like Stalin,
I used to spend hours in Makeup. To my astonishment, though, I have just found it, and watched it,
on Netflix. It wasn't as bad as I'd thought it would
be. I wonder whether the critics who thought we
had been miscast were possibly a little boxed in by
the working-class roles Bob and I had played before,
and their ideas about who we were.

Of these three "real" people I played on film,
I only managed to come face-to-face with one of
them. Stalin was dead by the time I was playing
him. I was not allowed to visit Brian Reader in
prison. I did, however, go to dinner at his very
grand official residence with F. W. de Klerk. One
little thing I noticed that evening, which I had not
picked up from studying the tapes: he was a chain-
smoker, but clearly a private, secret one. De Klerk
chain-smoked through the meal but I had never
seen him smoking in interviews or in a single photograph. I now recalled, though, that I had often
seen him holding one hand behind his back. I

guessed he had got so used to hiding his cigarettes that it had become a habit even when he didn't have one. I put that into my characterisation: the hidden hand was a kind of reserve and withholding. De Klerk, in the end, always reminded me a little of President Gorbachev of Russia: both were key players in the dismantling of terrible, brutal regimes but both got left behind by the forces they helped to set in train.

I also met Kip Thorne, the American theoretical physicist on whom my character Dr. Brand in *Interstellar* is based. Kip was a technical adviser to the movie, and my character's office, including the algebraic equation around the walls, two foot high and forty foot long, was based on Kip's real office. When I saw it I asked Kip, "Is that a real equation?"

"Yes," he said.

"And did you solve it?" I asked.

"Yes," he said again, and smiled.

This lovely and normal-seeming guy had a mind like nothing I had ever known before. And although my character was not supposed to be him, just based on someone like him, that was what I tried to put into my performance: a sense that even people with the most complex and brilliant minds can still be what we think of as "normal." They speak in surprisingly simple sentences; they experience the same range of emotions as the rest of us; they love their families just like anyone else.

At the after-party for the European premiere of the movie, at the Odeon Leicester Square in London, Kip introduced me to an even more extraordinary mind, belonging to a unique person. I was walking along the corridor to the Gents and saw Kip walking towards me pushing a wheelchair. In it a tiny man was screwed into an almost impossible position, with his face in a quite singular grimace. "Michael, this is one of my closest friends," Kip said. "Stephen Hawking." I knew Stephen's story and that he had a brilliant mind trapped inside an almost completely paralysed body. He could communicate only through tapping out words using the one body part he still had control over: a muscle in his right cheek.

As I stood there, probably with my mouth hanging open a bit in awe, Stephen Hawking tapped out on his pad, "I'd like to meet your wife." My wife is a beautiful, intelligent and charming woman, so I could understand the request. Stephen followed that up with requests to meet my beautiful *Interstellar* co-stars, Jessica Chastain and Anne Hathaway, who were drinking cocktails in impossibly glamorous frocks on the other side of the room. I made the introductions and Stephen wound up having a conversation with them and completely ignoring

me. I saw that, despite our different intellectual ca-
pacities, he and I did have some things in common:
our desire to make the most of our lives and every
opportunity presented to us, and our deep appreciation of female beauty.

Whether I am playing a real person or not,
I will always try to observe real people who re-
semble my character in some way to help me to
research the part. For *Zulu*, I had lunch every
day in the officers' mess of the Grenadier Guards:
although I had had plenty of interaction with officers as a private in the army, I had never observed
them interacting with each other. As my character's privileged background was an important part
of his character, and as I hadn't had a privileged
background, I also decided to study the Duke of
Edinburgh, who was the most privileged person
I could think of. What I noticed was that he
walked with his hands behind his back. I figured
that he was so powerful, well guarded and well
attended-to that he didn't need his hands to defend himself or indeed to do anything at all. I
played the part with my hands behind my back. (I
have to warn you, though, that my brilliant characterisation was somewhat misunderstood: "Actor
playing Bromhead so bad doesn't even know what
to do with hands. Suggest you replace him," said
the telegram from the producers when they saw

the first rushes. They came around in the end but those were tense days.)

For the part of Frank in *Educating Rita*, I based my characterisation of an alcoholic university lecturer on three people. The first was the professor who loves Marlene Dietrich, unrequitedly, in *The Blue Angel*. The other two were friends: Robert Bolt, the writer of *A Man for All Seasons* and a great teacher, who had a particular way of talking and explaining; and my business partner Peter Langan, who behaved like an alcoholic of quite majestic proportions. Within five years, at the age of forty-seven, Peter was dead following a fire that he had started when drunk.

My performance as Jack Carter in *Get Carter* was based on a gangster I had known in my earlier life. Not that I ever told him that. In fact, when he told me he thought the film was a load of crap I just nodded and agreed with everything he said. If you've seen *Get Carter* you'll understand exactly why. And *Alfie* was based on a guy called Jimmy Buckley, a charismatic friend of mine who always got the girl and would have been perfect to play the part himself, except he was always too tired.

And even when I played Scrooge in *The Muppet Christmas Carol* I did my research. You have to play comedy seriously. That's what makes it funny. So I played Scrooge straight, as though I was playing him for the Royal Shakespeare Company at the National Theatre. I researched him by watching CNN and following the trials and tribulations of all the Wall Street cheats and embezzlers of the time. There were plenty of them, as there always seem to be.

More generally, I observe people all the time. In the early days it was on the bus and the Tube. Now it's in restaurants, at the airport, in the doctor's waiting room. But wherever and whenever it is, I'm looking out for mannerisms, listening in for turns of phrase and watching how people respond to each other. Not just the obvious: I'm seeing whether I can discover something new. Over the years I have become an expert at reading body language. I remember in the 1960s when Russian agents were being discovered all over the British establishment, Kim Philby was being interviewed on television and the journalist said, "Answer me truthfully, are you a Russian spy?"

Philby turned his gaze down into his lap, then up again, looked the interviewer straight in the eye and said, "No."

"He's lying," I said to myself. He put his head down to get his face ready, to prepare the correct face of innocence. If he had been telling the truth he would not have needed to do that, he would just have said no. And I was right.

We can probably all benefit sometimes from trying to understand what is going on in other people's heads, what the world looks like from their point of view and what their mannerisms and expressions are telling us. I always find it helps me to feel more sympathy for others, and reminds me of my own good fortune. Also it means, however long I'm kept waiting, I'm never bored because I've always got something useful to be doing. But the main point I am trying to make here is: whatever form it takes, do your homework!

👓 *Learn your lines*

Confidence comes from experience plus preparation. Experience and preparation are your safety net, your insurance against a freefall off the high-wire. They are what you need to conquer your nerves and relax into a great performance. If you don't yet have much experience, it's even more important to focus on the preparation. *Alfie* was a huge opportunity for me and I was terrified I was going to screw it up. The nerves don't show on screen, though, because I knew my lines like I knew how to spell my own name. But even now, after more than a hundred major movies, preparation is still crucial. I will still learn my lines until they're a reflex, until saying each line on its cue is as automatic as saying, "Bless you," to a sneeze. Any actor who wants their career to endure has to do the same.

To learn my lines I would always say them to myself over and over. Walking down the street. In the shower. Making my dinner. It was absolutely continuous. Once I knew my lines, I would re-arrange the furniture at home or in my hotel room to be how I imagined it might be on set, and mock up props and practise using them. Then I would go over my lines again, but adding in movement around the set. Once we were shoot-ing, I would go over my lines again and again in my dressing room between takes. Apart from anything else, it directed my nervous energy into useful activity, something I could control.

It's a matter of repetition. Not just the words, but the thoughts and the feelings behind them, and the gestures, mannerisms and movements that ac-company them. (Keep anything physical simple and logical so that it aids your memory rather than act-ing as another burden on it.) Over and over until your cue makes you say, feel and react to the whole cycle of events it sets in train.

All of the techniques that applied to learning lines for an audition apply again once you have the part. Say your lines out loud. Practise until the line sounds perfectly natural. Convince yourself, and don't be a pushover. Be hard on yourself. Keep asking for more. Remember, this preparation is the work. Know the rest of the dialogue but don't have someone read the other parts for you. Retain an element of surprise so that you can truly listen and react naturally on set. You will need to try your lines in different ways. Think through the various ways to express each thought. Work them all up, then decide on the one that strikes you as the most valid and commit to it. Keep the others ready, though—you may need them. And don't overlook the possibilities in a mundane-seeming line. A good test of a restaurant is how well it does the basics— the literal bread and butter. And a good test of an actor is how much meaning they can get out of a simple line.

OTHER ACTOR: Did you have a coat?

YOU: Yes, thank you.

There are so many possibilities here. Maybe your coat is your most valued possession and you're surprised and offended because the question implies that the other actor hasn't noticed it. Maybe you're ashamed of your tatty coat, and mortified that the other actor is going to examine and handle it. Perhaps you feel that the question is a passive-aggressive way of asking you to leave when you're having a great time, an insinuation that your current outfit is not appropriate so needs to be covered up, or a suggestion that you might not own a coat. Perhaps the question indicates the other actor is socially nervous and awkward, because it's the middle of summer and obviously you wouldn't have a coat. Whatever your interpretation, it should start showing in your eyes on the word "coat." There is no need for a line ever to be boring.

In the movies, you will probably do all of this before you have the chance to discuss the role with the director, or see the set, or meet your fellow actors. But don't make the mistake of imagining that, because there is so much you cannot know in advance, you might as well not prepare. Somehow it is much easier to change one well-planned course of action for another precise course of action on the spur of the moment than it is to turn a vague idea into a concrete one. And as you gain experience you will find that a lot of your best guesses about things you cannot know in advance turn out to be right.

The goal of all of this preparation is that by the time you get to the set you will have reduced the chances of something going wrong from high to remote, and transformed your mental state from abject terror to clear-headed readiness. I am never worried that I might forget my lines, so the energy I could have spent worrying over that, I can instead put into really listening to the people I'm acting with (of which more later), and into flexing my performance to cope with whatever sweat-inducing matters arise on that particular day. Because I'm prepared, I can perform at my best.

I might, for example, need to put my energy into reacting to a director's vision. I will turn up to a film set not only having learnt my lines but also having taken countless decisions about how I'm going to play them: pace, pauses, gestures, emphases. When you are about to be called to the set to discover the director's intentions for you, terror can strike all too easily. Knowing that you know your lines—and that, should your favoured interpretation not cut the mustard with the director, you have some alternatives in your back pocket—helps to keep the heart beating at a normal pace and the terror level somewhere below abject. My brain can make the leap the director is asking me to make, because it is not having to work to remember what I'm going to say.

The next day I might need to react to a director altering the script at a moment's notice, or changing his mind mid-shoot about how he wants a scene to play. I might need to keep my nerve and behave as though I'm getting exactly what I want from another actor, even when I'm not. The director might even ask me to improvise. (This doesn't happen much: directors are notorious control freaks. But I did enjoy ad-libbing the supermarket scene in *The Ipcress File*, where my character Harry Palmer is shopping for food to make dinner for a woman he wants to seduce while talking to the spy master, who is also pushing a supermarket trolley, and the very funny scene where I was drilling local recruits, including one spectacular incompetent, in *The Man Who Would Be King*.)

Or I might just be dealing with really challenging working conditions. If I know my lines back to front, I can still deliver exactly what the director requires of me in searing heat, wearing a crippling costume and surrounded by a distracting crowd of locals, determined to take in the bizarre and fascinating circus that has come to town.

And, by the way, don't do what I did and only prep for today's scenes. Plan ahead for tomorrow, and the days after that too. Learn your lines for the whole film before you start shooting, and keep studying whenever you get a break. I got caught on that once, early in my career, and never made the mistake again. In 1971 I was shooting *Kidnapped*, an adventure film based on Robert Louis Stevenson's book. We were on location on the Isle of Mull off the west coast of Scotland and, for once, the weather conditions were perfect. So much so that at lunchtime the director, Delbert Mann, announced, "The light is brilliant. I want to shoot your last scene this afternoon."

"We aren't scheduled to shoot that scene today, Delbert," I said, panic rising in my throat and tightening my chest. My last scene was an extensive soliloquy about my deep feelings for Scotland and I hadn't even looked at it.

"Michael, we have to use the weather," said Delbert. "I want to shoot it after lunch."

"Give me an hour," I said. Lunch was abandoned as I holed myself up in my trailer.

In the end I did it in one take. But I would have saved myself an hour of anguish if I'd prepared all my lines before the shoot began—if I'd thought ahead and given myself the ability to be flexible as plans changed. (Mind you, I would have saved myself several weeks of anguish if I hadn't made the picture at all. It was a dud, and the only film I've never been paid for.)

∞ Be like a duck

Ducks look calm as they glide along the surface of the water but they're paddling like hell underneath. When you're doing your preparation right, it sometimes looks so good that people watching you make the mistake of assuming it's all natural and effortless. In my experience, it never is. Some of the most "natural" performers are the hardest-working, and some of the most apparently spontaneous performances are the ones that have been the best-rehearsed. To get to a natural performance you have to go right through acting and come out the other side into real, and that's a long, tough journey, underground, with no scenery.

In 1984, Woody Allen directed the movie *Hannah and Her Sisters*. The movie was a commercial and critical success and my performance in it as Elliot won me my first Academy Award. His films appear very naturalistic, and it would be easy to believe that parts of the dialogue are ad-libbed. The truth is the precise opposite. It takes an enormous amount of work to achieve the levels of naturalism that Woody does. He works on his scripts for months before a shoot, and the dialogue is then carved in stone unless you can come up with something better than the material he has spent months perfecting. Which you can't.

Once everyone is on set, everything is very deliberate and calm and he rehearses exhaustively, with almost no distinction between the energy of the rehearsal and the energy of the take, which makes for relaxed actors with a very naturalistic kind of energy. He also has an incredible eye for detail and minutiae, knows exactly what he wants and will work quietly but relentlessly until he has it. For example, one day I did a rehearsal, then a take. Woody cut it and asked, "Why didn't you do that movement with your hand that you did in the rehearsal?" I had no idea what I'd done with my hand but he showed me and we shot it again. Other times he would just say, "Do it again, Michael." I would do it again and he would say, "Yes, that's it. Print." I wouldn't know what was different, but he would have seen some tiny thing. (The allegations about Woody Allen have come as a great and terrible shock to me. The Woody I knew was kind and gentle and I learnt a great deal from his craft.)

In 1988 I made a movie called *Without a Clue* in which I played a comedic Sherlock Holmes to Ben Kingsley's Dr. Watson. The producer, Mark Sturdivant, observed Ben and me on set and decided that we were two very different kinds of actors. I remember he reported that "Michael is very instinctive, Ben is very intellectual." As evidence for this he described how, during a read-through, someone would call out, "Scene ninety," and Ben would instantly be going through the script, checking what had happened to his character before, so that he could get into the right frame of mind. "Meanwhile, Michael would be slumped on the couch, picking balls of fluff off of his sweater."

I'm not claiming that my Sherlock Holmes was one of my best or most naturalistic performances. But Mark had got me wrong. It wasn't that it was all instinctive. It was that I had already done my thinking. I already knew what my frame of mind was in scene ninety. The rehearsal I had done on my own, before arriving at the set, was the thinking, the working. Now that we were on set, this was the performance and I was doing my relaxing.

Movie acting is a delicate blend of preparation and spontaneity. If you do enough preparation, you can put in a performance that appears brilliantly instinctive and natural. The same goes for most performance, in the widest sense of the word. All of us have to perform at times. Far from destroying spontaneity, careful and thorough preparation will enable it. When you have learnt your lines, when you know your stuff, you have the firm foundation you need to be your best and to listen and react truthfully in the moment.

7.

Less Is More

"I told you. You're only sup-posed to blow the bloody doors off."

The Italian Job, 1969

LIKE I SAID BEFORE, whatever role you're performing in life, you have to know your craft. So, at the moment when the cameras roll and the director shouts, "Action!," what do you really need to know? In movie acting, it's a lot of little technical things, and two great big things: you have to listen and react; and you have to be real.

👓 *My tricks of the trade*

In any walk of life, there are the big lessons, and then there are the little tricks of the trade that no one ever tells you and that can give you that extra edge. Well, I'm going to tell you my little tricks of the trade. Most of them are about the ways we use our bodies and our voices to make an impact. That's crucial in my trade but also comes in quite handy in all kinds of other scenarios.

If you get the big things right, your acting will come out through your eyes. (And, by the way, this is impossible if your eyes are rolled backwards in your head, searching your brain for your next line. You have to know your line so well that you can say it as if you're minting it fresh, not hauling it out of your memory. Did I mention that it's important to learn your lines?)

When I'm doing a close-up, I make sure I don't switch my lead focus from one eye to the other. The camera will pick up the tiny eye movement and it will make me look shifty. Marlene Dietrich taught me that, at a party. (How to choose which eye? Choose the off-camera actor's eye that is closest to the camera, and look at it with your eye that is furthest from the camera. That will keep you in eye contact with the off-camera actor, but also put your full face in shot.)

In real life, when we're listening closely to someone, we might not keep eye contact endlessly (that would be unnerving) but we don't flick our gaze all over the room. If we do, the other person quickly gets the message that something more interesting is going on over their shoulder.

When you blink on camera, especially in close-up when every blink is eight feet wide, it makes you look weak. Look at Hugh Grant blinking away in his romantic-comedy roles, then contrast with his more recent, brilliant portrayal of Jeremy Thorpe in *A Very English Scandal*—when I don't think he blinks once—if you want the proof of that. So, I try not to blink, unless I'm supposed to be weak, or shocked or concerned, or have something in my eye. (Try this at home if you want to come across more assertively. Don't take it too far, though: you'll upset your friends or contract an eye infection.)

I never look down to find my mark, because then the camera loses my eyes. Instead I work out beforehand exactly where it is, then sense it with my peripheral vision. Spencer Tracy, indirectly, taught me that. Watch him and you'll see that he walks, looks down, then speaks. That's because he's always looking for his mark. If you have to hold an important conversation, make sure you can focus on that, and are not going to be distracted by having to shuffle around to find the right piece of paper, or whatever your particular "finding your mark" is.

I don't overreact. From observing people experiencing enormous emotion in real life I have learnt that in times of great stress or disaster, and often even in times of great joy, we don't react immediately. There is usually a moment or two of blankness while we register the shock. Only after that do we start to get to grips with our new world.

Unless I have to do an accent because that's part of the performance, I stick with my usual voice. When I was playing German characters in *The Last*

Valley and *The Eagle Has Landed*, or Stalin in *Then There Were Giants*, or Wilbur Larch in *The Cider House Rules*, the accent was part of the performance. I always prefer to use my own voice because focusing on an accent will take at least 50 per cent of my concentration, which would be more usefully directed somewhere else. In any encounter, the energy and effort you put into hiding your true self is energy and effort that could probably be put to better use. There are times for all of us when we elect to be less than fully authentic to fit in, but when you can, take pride in being precisely yourself.

Accent or no accent, I would advise everybody to learn how to produce their voice correctly. Breathe from the diaphragm: it's right down there, below your lungs and above your stomach. There's a technique to it, which my first wife taught me. Cockneys tend to speak from up there, stuck in their throat, which makes for a completely different kind of sound. When you produce from your diaphragm, your sound will be richer, and more versatile. That—not speaking the Queen's English—is what will make your voice comfortable to listen to.

👓 *Be real*

My biggest single piece of advice to someone wanting to know how to do movie acting—and, in fact, to anyone wanting to make a good impression, or feeling they have to perform in some way—would be this: be real. Don't act. Don't perform. "Performing" works in the theatre, where everything has to be big and broad, and you have to project your voice to reach the back row even in the quiet scenes. But in the movies, where the camera picks up every tiny blink and twitch, and the microphone picks up every whisper, "acting" or "performing" will blow your cover and spoil the illusion. Now you look like someone being paid to say their lines, someone trying to smash it out of the park, rather than a real person thinking real thoughts and living their real life. You have lost your credibility, your believability. In the movies, everything has to be small and natural. Movie actors who "act" are always obvious and fail to convince.

To be real in front of the camera, you have to be so in tune with the life of your character that you're thinking his or her thoughts. You are not you-pretending-to-be-him. Or you are, at some level. That's unavoidable. But at another level, you just *are* him.

The careful observation you have done as part of

your preparation will help: the thought you have already put into things like how you walk, how you hold yourself, what you do with your hands, how you use your voice. Powerful people walk from their centre with purpose and ease. Slouch, stoop, poke your head forward, and your power dissolves. Stand straight and you look younger; round your shoulders for instant ageing. Talking slowly can imply power—because you know people will stop and listen to you—or dishonesty: you work out the lies as you go along. Hands can show a tremendous amount of character. A tiny hand gesture can convey neuroticism or nerves much more effectively than urgent pacing to and fro or a physically demanding pratfall. Those physical decisions, with your costume, hair and makeup, can really help you change your mental state.

Similarly, if you're looking for a promotion at work, it can be helpful to observe the people you want to be. How do they behave? Don't go overboard. Your co-workers will think you're taking the piss if you start walking around imitating your boss. But little changes in behaviour can start to help you to see yourself in a different light. And that is the first step to making others see you in that light too.

Deep empathy will also help you to be real. As an actor, you have to understand who your character is and what they do from inside their heads. Jack Carter in *Get Carter* and Harry Brown in *Harry Brown* both go on nasty killing sprees. People are dropped off the sides of buildings, drowned inside car boots, or lectured while they bleed out from stomach wounds. But neither Jack nor Harry is a psychopath. From inside their own heads, they have their reasons for what they're doing. In real life, everyone is in sympathy with his own motives. Jack is defending his family's honour—a concept that is every bit as important to him as it is to members of the British aristocracy or the Sicilian Mafia. Harry is seeking vengeance for his friend's senseless death, scaring the people who scare him and cleaning up his estate of a bunch of undesirable gangsters and drug dealers. To them, they're doing the right thing, killing people who deserve to be killed. Even Joseph Stalin made sense to himself.

Funnily enough it was not the murderous hard men I had the most difficulty empathising with. The biggest challenge for me was when I was cast completely against type in *The Romantic Englishwoman* as Lewis Fielding, a rather ineffective and passive pseudo-intellectual wimp who lets his life fall apart all around him. Lewis's wife, played by Glenda Jackson, goes off on a romantic adventure and he does nothing to stop her. I managed then by trying to imagine what I *wouldn't* do in any given situation, and then having Lewis do exactly that.

We can intellectualise empathy. We have to think through our characters' motivations. But to *feel* the emotion I have decided my character is going to feel at any given point, I rely on sense memory, going back to my own real-life experiences to access emotion, as taught to me by Joan Littlewood.

For rage, I go back to when I was evacuated as a child and locked in a cupboard. I instantly feel a hatred of all adults and, bang!, I'm on the rampage. For fear, I remember Korea, being surrounded by the enemy and certain I was going to die.

Unfortunately for me, but fortunately for my acting career, I have a wide choice of memories I can call on when I have to cry: walking away from my first marriage when my elder daughter Dominique was a baby; being told when she was a few hours old that my younger daughter Natasha had a 50 per cent chance of making it; sitting there for two weeks with her tiny hand gripping the finger I had managed to slip through the little hole in the side of her incubator. There's also a memory I go into that is so personal I haven't even told my wife about it. I worry that if I tell her, the memory will be lost: it will be mixed up with my memory of her reaction to it. So I've held that one close.

And, most of all, what will help you to be real

and truthful in your performance is doing less, not more.

In *Educating Rita*, I remembered my old repertory director's advice about playing a drunk. Watch Frank in that movie and you'll see that he isn't reeling and staggering around. It's smaller than that. He's struggling to appear sober, fighting to maintain his dignity. What gives him away is what gives all drunks away. You can see in his eyes that his thought processes are slowed. Everything in the chain of listening, thinking, speaking is getting delayed. And you can see from the way he is holding himself that his muscle tone is compromised. It takes a supreme effort to make his neck hold up his head and stop it dropping onto his chest.

That director from Lowestoft Rep gave me the same advice about crying. "You, Michael," he said, after he had stopped me once more and asked me what on earth I thought I was doing, "are giving me an actor trying to cry. I want a real man. A real man is someone who is trying desperately *not* to cry." Spot on. In real life people tend not to turn on the waterworks in a great grief-stricken dramatic way. So when we're acting it's more truthful and more powerful to fight the emotion, to struggle with the feelings, to hide the tears.

Some actors will try to steal a scene by being bigger and louder than everyone else. (Or sometimes they're slumming it from the theatre and haven't adjusted. That's true particularly for the post-war generation of actors who do a film to buy a new car, then return to their art.) Their gestures are semaphore. Their lines are bellowed proclamations. These actors are using their bodies and voices rather than their brains. Don't try to compete. Do your thing and come in underneath them. When they go big, you go small. When they shout and scream and pull faces, you stay centred and calm. They are the ones who will end up looking stupid.

Put it another way. Don't blow up the whole car. No one needs that. You're only supposed to blow the bloody doors off.

As in life, quite how small you make it will depend on the set-up. In the movies, there are master shots (or long shots), medium shots and close-ups. The closer the camera, the smaller your performance needs to be. The same in life. You can afford to be a bit bigger when you're addressing a roomful of people, but the general point still applies. You will have more impact if you pare things back—your reactions, your presentation, your interventions. Avoid being loud or grandiose or verbose. Remember how devastating and impactful one perfectly nuanced inflection or expression can be. People can interpret and infer more than we realise without us needing to over-stress. Stay interesting and stay real.

Jack Lemmon told me this story when I first went to Hollywood. In his first film he was being directed by George Cukor, and in his first scene, Cukor kept cutting as soon as he started speaking. "Do less, Jack," George said. He started again and George cut it again. "Do less, Jack." They did the scene over and over, with Jack doing less and less each time. Finally George cut again and asked Jack to do less again and Jack said, "If I do any less I'll be doing nothing."

"Now you've got it, Jack," said George.

It needs to be very small, but it's not nothing. Do not make the mistake of thinking that being natural is doing nothing. The effort is huge. The intensity is huge. Your brain is in overdrive, thinking every moment. You are working very hard to get through acting and out the other side back to reality.

When I was coming up the people who did this brilliantly were Henry Fonda in *The Grapes of Wrath* and Marlon Brando in *On the Waterfront.* At that time their more relaxed and underplayed acting style was revolutionary and a revelation to people like me in the audience. Clark Gable had always played Clark Gable, Robert Taylor was always Robert Taylor and Charles Boyer was always Charles Boyer. Now the naturalistic acting style is the norm. We don't want our movie actors to be big orating stars. And we don't want them always to be glamorous versions of themselves. None of the parts I have played—not Alfie, Harry Palmer from *The Ipcress File* or Harry Brown, any more than Wilbur Larch in *The Cider House Rules* or Thomas Fowler in *The Quiet American*—have been me. They have all been people I knew, not people I am. We want our movie actors to be real other people. You can watch brilliant examples of this real style of acting every day now, but if you really want to learn from the best, I'd take a look at Benedict Cumberbatch giving an extraordinary performance in *Patrick Melrose*, or Gemma Arterton, or Idris Elba, or Clare Foy, or Hugh Grant, or Tom Hiddleston, or Lily James, or Damien Lewis, or Matt Smith. This is a difficult industry and you never know what will happen but they're all wonderful screen actors, and they all have star quality.

👓 *The art of listening*

When I'm learning my lines, I put as much thought into the parts where I'm not speaking as I do into the parts where I am. Sometimes more.

Remember that wise old director from my repertory days in Lowestoft? The one who was always stopping me to tell me what I was doing wrong? One day we were rehearsing and he called for us to stop. "What are you doing in this scene, Michael?" he asked.

"Nothing," I said, slightly indignantly. "I haven't got anything to say for ages." I couldn't see how I could possibly be doing anything wrong this time, because I didn't have any lines at all.

"That, Michael," said the director, "is where you're wrong. Of course you have something to say. You are listening to what is being said, and thinking of a thousand wonderful things to say. You are standing there and thinking these wonderful thoughts. And you are deciding not to say any of them. Half of acting is listening. And the other half is reacting. Listening and reacting," he said, "not 'nothing,' is what you are doing in this scene."

It was great advice. Listen and react. Don't stand there thinking about your next line. Don't stand there thinking about nothing. Really listen to what the other person is saying. Really tune in to what they're doing. (And don't move about: people don't move about when they're really listening.) And then give a truthful reaction.

Escape to Victory is John Huston's 1981 cult classic about a group of Allied prisoners of war trying to break free from their captors while preparing for an exhibition soccer game against them. I had enormous fun shooting that movie. Sly Stallone co-starred as the goalkeeper, my hero John Huston was directing and I got to play football alongside footballing giants Pelé, the Brazilian football genius, Bobby Moore, who had captained the England 1966 World Cup winning team, and Argentina's Ossie Ardiles. It was like a dream come true. There's one little scene where Pelé—playing one of the prisoners of war—starts to play with the ball, and I, as Captain John Colby, the captain and coach of the PoW team, first realise he has some skills. On paper, I do nothing in that scene until the end, when I have one line: "Where'd you learn to do that?" But if you watch the scene you'll see that while Pelé is doing what he does best, picking up the ball with the top of his foot then bouncing it from his foot to his shoulder to his head, I am doing my thing, with the saying nothing. I'm not just standing there. I'm noticing him. I'm watching him with growing interest. My mind is turning over what I'm seeing and what it means. What I am definitely not doing is standing there doing nothing.

In life, we don't listen blankly to someone else making a speech with no thoughts in our heads, simply waiting for them to stop so that we can say our piece. And we don't interrupt every time we do have an interesting thought. Or if we do, we don't end up with many friends. In life, we are always thinking our thousands of wonderful thoughts, and the thought that inspires our next words usually occurs when the other person is still speaking, often provoked by something they're saying.

OTHER ACTOR: I'm going out to meet Freda. I'll back in an hour or two but don't wait up.

YOU: Freda? Really? That's funny. She just called me to ask why you had cancelled.

The key word here is "Freda." When the other actor says "Freda," that sets off your next thoughts: How can she be going to meet Freda, when Freda just told me she had cancelled? Why is she lying to me? And so on. The other actor doesn't stop talking at "Freda," so you don't start talking then. But you can show by your reaction—not a dramatic gasp, but a microscopic tightening of the jaw, a lowering of the eyes perhaps, it depends on what you're trying to convey—that you already know what you're going to say next. Realistic performance comes from intense listening and truthful reaction.

In the movies, you earn your living and learn your craft by listening. To the extent that a lot of experienced actors actually try to cut down their dialogue, rather than counting their lines as theatre actors tend to do. Look at Sylvester Stallone as Rambo, or Scarlett Johansson in *Under the Skin*, or Leonardo DiCaprio in *The Revenant*. Look at Sally Hawkins in 2018's Oscar-winning movie *The Shape of Water*. A hugely impactful performance with no spoken lines at all.

Or look at me as Frank in *Educating Rita*. I had been Alfie in *Alfie*, and Jack Carter in *Get Carter*. A lot of my friends thought I was mad to be in a film that was about someone called Rita. But I knew that at the heart of this story there was a relationship between two people, and that even if Julie Walters, as Rita, had the most lines, and did most of the moving about—and a quite superb job she made of it too—a lot of the dramatic interest would come from cutting to a sedentary Frank for his reactions.

Once again, less is more. In movie acting, as in life, you don't have to be saying a lot to be effective. In movie acting, as in life, the real value is not in how you say your own lines but in how you listen and react truthfully in the moment to what other people are saying to you.

8.

Having Serious Fun

"Not many people know that."

Educating Rita, 1983

ABOVE AND BEYOND YOUR craft there are some characteristics that come in very handy if you want to succeed in the movies or anywhere else. You are going to need stamina, flexibility, the ability to focus completely and the ability (at the same time) to relax and have fun. The last one isn't strictly necessary but it definitely makes life easier for you and for everyone around you.

👓 *Finding your inner strength*

One day, in the middle of a tough shoot in a difficult location, the assistant director announced that as we had fallen behind schedule we would be shooting for an extra three hours that day. "But it's one hundred degrees in the shade," I protested.

"Well, stay out of the fucking shade, then," suggested the AD.

Shooting a movie can be physically and mentally gruelling and you have to be prepared for a long, tough haul. There might be night shooting—four pages of dialogue at three in the morning—followed by a dawn call for hair and makeup the following day. The location might be freezing tundra, a dripping jungle or a dull, cold, unfriendly city with nowhere to get a decent meal. Your shoes might pinch: costume shoes never seem to fit properly. There will almost certainly be a lot of waiting around, expending nervous energy, before you're suddenly needed, hitting all the right notes perfectly and first time out.

Most things in life that are worth doing require similar mental or physical reserves, so build up your stamina and your resilience. Be prepared for boredom and discomfort, and find ways to manage them. Don't complain about the less glamorous bits of your job. Don't fret if you're all dressed up with nowhere to go: believe that your moment will come, stay ready for it and keep thinking about your next move.

Everyone has their own strategy for dealing with "dead time." Some people sleep. But watch out: you don't want to appear groggy and slow when you come round. Some get lost in their smartphones, but don't become so engrossed in the world of your phone that your real role in the real world starts to feel like a distraction. Sylvester Stallone used to do sit-ups if he got a five-minute break, sit-ups and push-ups if he got ten minutes. I lost weight just watching him. In the longer breaks, Sly would disappear off to his trailer. I wondered whether he had a woman in there, or perhaps a personal trainer, and finally I asked him what was so attractive about his trailer. "I'm writing *Rocky III*," he said. I don't like to split my attention like that. Guess what I do in my trailer? I prepare my next scene. I go over my lines. Occasionally a technician asks me, "Don't you get bored, just hanging around?" They're making the same mistake I made back in Lowestoft. I'm not just hanging around. I'm hanging around preparing for what's coming next.

👓 *When stuff happens, be flexible*

Despite all the preparation you will have done, things will not go to plan. Maybe the writer's lines don't work in the set the scenic designers have come up with, or the writer didn't take into account the physical reality of the shoot location, so the lines have to be changed. Maybe the director has had a genius new idea overnight and is bursting to try it out. Maybe he has decided to throw the script out of the window.

The director Sidney Furie literally set fire to his script on the first day of the shoot for *The Ipcress File*, announcing to the assembled cast and crew, "That's what I think of that." I suppose he was telling us that we were not going to be tied to the script. We all stood around, stealing worried looks at each other, baffled as to what we were going to shoot. Then Sidney turned to me and said, "Oh, what the hell. Give me your script." I handed it over. No problem, of course, because I knew my lines. "Now let's get to work." Once everyone had taken a breath we got on with the shoot, including a fair amount of improvisation, and made what turned out to be one of Sidney's best movies.

Stuff happens. Try not to react to any of it with blank horror. Panic is prohibited. Whatever it is, you have to take it in your stride—which you will be able to do because, of course, you're so thoroughly prepared. You have practised and prepared several interpretations. You know your lines so well that adding in a couple more or fiddling about with one or two is child's play. Your mind is hanging loose enough to make the leap to where it needs to go.

👓 Staying focused

When you're on, you're on, and it's crucial that you stay in the moment. Because the camera picks up everything, it is enormously important to maintain total concentration during your take, especially during a close-up. To listen and react truthfully, to find the real emotion, your brain will be working double-time. If your attention strays even for a moment—if you hesitate over your line for just a fraction of a second, if your eyes flicker because off-camera someone walks across your sight-line, if you're thinking about what you're going to have for lunch, or the last shot, or the next shot—the camera will catch it.

One of the times I found it most challenging to concentrate was when we were shooting *Alfie*. I had to run out into Notting Hill Gate, a busy street in west London. These days Notting Hill is full of creative types but this was pre-gentrification and Notting Hill was a lot more earthy back then. My line was "Darling! Come back! I love you!" and the people who had started to gather round to see what was going on in their neighbourhood evidently found this quite amusing. They started to heckle me, quite creatively. (Maybe there were more creative types round there back then than I realised.) The director told me to carry on and he would post-synch the sound in later. I just had to block it out, and keep my focus.

But most of the time I don't have any difficulty concentrating. I have trained myself to think only about the shot and to be completely in the moment, isolated from whatever madness might be going on around me. It's hard to give instructions for how to do this, to articulate what is going on in my brain when I'm blocking out everything else, except that, like most things, it gets better with practice.

In life, as in front of a camera, your audience will know when your attention strays. When you're only half concentrating on the meeting. When you're only three-quarters listening to your partner. In life, as in front of a camera, if you focus completely on what you're doing right now, you will stay truthful and have more impact.

👓 Relaxing and having fun

Don't forget that, while you're achieving this intense focus and concentration, you also need to be achieving relaxation. It is this combination that will allow you to give your very best performance.

I was not always a relaxed performer. I have already mentioned the bucket I used to have to keep in the wings when I first started performing on stage. Later, when I first got tiny parts in movies, the deafening silence that followed the call of "Quiet!" on a movie set used to throw me into such a state of nervous collapse about my one line that to my intense mortification I often messed it up.

Come to think of it, I was also extremely nervous on my first big movie. My first day shooting dialogue on location for *Zulu* was not designed to put me at my ease, and if I want to summon up a sense memory of nervous exhaustion and near-hysterical tension, I go back to that time. My heavy wool uniform was hot and uncomfortable under the intense South African sun. The upper-class British accent I had assured Cy Endfield would be no trouble at all was taking up half of my focus. The horse that had spent the previous day playing silly buggers was delighted to see me again, and had thrown me in the river three times, each time requiring a change of clothes. Staying on his back was taking the other half of my focus. Finally I managed to walk the horse up to Stanley Baker and get out my line: "Hot day, hard work."

"CUT!" shouted Cy. "Michael, why is your voice so high?"

I protested that this was just my normal voice, like I'd used in rehearsal, so he had the sound technician play it back. Then I heard it. I was so nervous that my shoulders had tensed and my throat had tightened and as a result I had transformed myself from an effete but convincing tenor to a shrieking soprano. The horse and I had to cross that river one more time, I had to force myself to relax—which, as anyone who has ever been urged to "just relax" will tell you, is extremely difficult—and finally I nailed the line.

Now I'm always relaxed on set. So much so that occasionally I even fall asleep. Alan Arkin likes to tell the story of being on set and walking past me dozing off like a pensioner on a deckchair. It must have been a slight worry for the director, Zach Braff, seeing one of his stars comatose. Or maybe he didn't spot me. Because what Alan also says is that the next thing Zach was yelling, "Action!" and off I went like a bomb. "There was no transition. He went from snoring to being 120 per cent ready. I just couldn't believe it. It was like a thoroughbred at the starting gate." I don't know about thoroughbreds. Some might say I'm not far off the knacker's yard. But I do still know my way around the racetrack.

In general I would say relax, but don't get so relaxed you fall asleep. If you're asleep on the job, you can't expect the audience to stay awake.

Some actors work out of tension rather than relaxation. It's OK for them, I guess, but it does put a strain on everyone around them. They get everyone wound up and upset and then they're ready to go. I'm the opposite. I'm laughing and cracking jokes until the last minute, even if in the scene I'm going to cry. Then I finish the scene and I'm back to cracking jokes.

My top tip for dealing with nerves? Preparation,

of course. Experience helps too. Knowing you've done it before, tackled difficult things in the past and got through them, gives you confidence that you can do it again. (The importance of experience was brought home to me recently when I was asked to do a poetry reading in Westminster Abbey. Even thinking about it brought me out in hives. I was back to my old stage fright and the bucket in the wings. It wasn't the grandeur of the building or the occasion. It was my lack of experience. I had barely ever read a poem and certainly had never recited any in public. I said, "Thank you very much for asking but I'd rather not have a nervous breakdown in Westminster Abbey.")

I usually do relaxation exercises before difficult scenes as well. Take a deep breath in, then bend over with your arms dangling loose and your legs a little bit bent and enjoy the blood rushing to your head. Straighten up slowly while you breathe out. Take three deep breaths. You should feel more relaxed, more focused and more in control. The only time I wouldn't do this is if I'm supposed to be nervous in the scene. Then I skip the relaxation exercises and have a double espresso instead.

When I was in *Sleuth* with Laurence Olivier, the most difficult scene was the one when my character thinks that Larry's character is going to kill him, and begs for mercy, beside himself with terror. I

had starred in a lot of films by this time, but playing opposite Laurence Olivier was somewhat nerve-
racking so I was actually more nervous than usual
and I deliberately, for this scene, did not try to calm
my nerves. My disintegration into a jabbering mess,
begging for my life, was pretty convincing, including to me. And, evidently, to Lord Olivier. As we
walked back to the dressing rooms, Larry came up
and put his arm round me. "When we started this
film," he said confidentially, "I thought of you as
a talented assistant." He left a dramatic pause, à la
Olivier. "But now I see that I have a partner." I
don't think I have ever received a compliment that
has meant more.

I only once resorted to alcohol to deal with nerves
and it was a special case. I was doing *Deathtrap*, the
1982 *Sleuth*-like thriller in which I played opposite
Christopher Reeve as his lover and the two of us plot-
ted together to kill my wife. There was a scene in
which we had to kiss each other passionately and
never having kissed a man before—except my dad,
on his cheek—I was finding it hard to psych myself
up to it. I tried convincing myself it was an honour
to kiss Superman. I was nervous as hell. In the end we
got through it not with breathing exercises but with
a bottle of brandy between us. We nailed the kiss but
were both so drunk we couldn't remember our lines.

*   *   *

I do like to laugh. I remember Roger Moore, years ago, saying to me, "Cheer up. You'd better have a good time because this is not a rehearsal, this is life—this is the show."

Taking the work seriously doesn't mean you can't have any fun. Quite the opposite. I usually find things go better when everyone's having a good time. Some actors are always worrying, always complaining. They're what I call "losing the light" actors. For them, if it isn't perfect, it's all spoilt. It's a bad script; or a good script but the director doesn't know how to treat it; or the script is OK and the director's great but the other actors have all been miscast. And, incidentally, the lighting is all wrong and they don't have enough lines. I come from another school of thought. In this school we have more fun, and we get more done. We're invigorated and entertained by the challenges that each day brings. We take pleasure in either moving the inevitable stumbling blocks out of the way, or finding a way to dodge around them. We feel so privileged to be part of the game that we keep playing long after all the light has gone and it's time for bed.

Doing serious work doesn't mean you can't have any fun either. Making a comedy can turn into a gruelling slog if you get actors and crew with the wrong attitudes; but by the same token, with the right people, making a serious piece can be a scream. Anthony Hopkins told me that he had never had more laughs on set than when he was making the terrifying horror film *The Silence of the Lambs* with Jodie Foster.

It's hard for me to narrow down which movies I've had the most fun making. *The Man Who Would Be King* was wonderful fun because Sean Connery and I had such good on-screen chemistry and John Huston gave us the freedom to run with it. The atmosphere on set was very special. However, the chronic diarrhoea I suffered throughout the shoot in Morocco did reduce the spring in my step a little. I had a party making *Bullseye*, with Roger Moore and Michael Winner, but a terrible hangover when the movie came out and flopped. A very strong contender would have to be *Dirty Rotten Scoundrels*, shot in my dream location within close reach of many excellent restaurants and beaches. There was one scene with Glenne Headly, a terrific actress who sadly died at just sixty-two, that we had to shoot fifty times: we just couldn't stop laughing.

It's also important to be able to laugh at yourself. Take your work seriously, yes, but don't whatever you do get all pompous and start taking *yourself* too seriously. It's fortunate that this has never been a problem for me. Peter Sellers started taking the mickey with the "Not many people know that" line. He was obsessed with gadgets and he had one of the first answering machines. I phoned him one day and his message was an impersonation of me saying, "Dis is Michael Caine speaking. Peter Sellers is out. Not many people know that." Little sod. Then in about 1972 he did it on *Parkinson*, which was the most popular chat-show at the time. I got in on the joke myself in *Educating Rita*, where my character said the line, kind of as an in-joke. Not many people know that. It was also me going "My name is Michael Caine" on the 1984 Madness track "My Name Is Michael Caine." My daughter Natasha, who was eleven years old at the time, really liked Madness and she persuaded me to do it.

Paul Whitehouse did a rip-off of me as Harry Palmer in *Harry Enfield's Television Programme*, going, "My name is Michael Paine, and I am a nosy neighbour." And now Rob Brydon and Steve Coogan have revived it all again in *The Trip* when they bicker with each other about who can do the best Michael Caine impressions. I think it's bloody hilarious. Although the best Michael Caine impression I've heard is Tom Hanks's: he did it on *Saturday Night Live*. I was surprised because I know Tom Hanks and—unlike almost everyone else I ever meet—he'd never done the impression for me.

Luckily I don't ever get tired of people quoting myself at me. So long as it doesn't make me sound like too much of a moron. In fact, these days, I quote myself back again. I can do an excellent Michael Caine impression. "My name...is Michael Caine." See?

Can you ever have too much fun at work? I can think of a couple of ways. If you're laughing so much you can't get any work done (in acting we call it corpsing) the director is going to shut the party down pretty quickly.

And you don't want to have too much of the wrong kind of fun with your leading lady. Or any other cast member. Movies are notoriously bad for marriages. First of all, you're away from each other for long stretches. There's a saying in the movies, "Location doesn't count," but look at the movie divorce rate and you will see that this rule does not always apply. You go away on location for three months, maybe somewhere exciting and glamorous, and your partner stays at home, and when you get back you've had a great time and made a load of new friends, and she's had a great time and made a load of new friends, and you're kind of strangers. That puts a strain on a marriage. Then in the movies you're often being paid to kiss and cuddle your fabulous new friends, or even to get into bed and pretend to make love to them. This is where you have to abandon method acting, and keep things extremely professional. It will save your marriage and it will save the movie. The point goes more widely, of course: in any walk of life, don't confuse having fun with being unprofessional or disrespectful of your colleagues, and don't act in a way that might allow your professional reputation to be undermined by unwelcome gossip.

My long marriage to Shakira has survived for two reasons. First, I married the most beautiful, intelligent, kind and all-round-wonderful person in the world. And, second, Shakira always came with me on location. Not so much to keep an eye on me, or for me to keep an eye on her, but so that our lives would stay intertwined.

There is a myth that film stars are all demanding divas. If that was ever true it isn't now. There are too many talented people around for anyone to be prepared to put up with that kind of nonsense for long. All things being equal, film people prefer the actor who turns up on time, knows his lines, is fun to work with and stays focused on the task in hand. In life, as in the movies, competence is a basic and yet all-too-rare quality. Never underestimate its value. Most people will pick competent professionalism over erratic brilliance any day of the week.

9.

Taking Direction

Ebenezer Scrooge: "Let us deal with the eviction notices for tomorrow, Mr. Cratchit."
Kermit the Frog: "Uh, tomorrow's Christmas, sir."
Ebenezer Scrooge: "Very well. You may gift wrap them."

The Muppet Christmas Carol, 1992

MOVIE ACTORS ARE EXPECTED to fully pre-pare their roles before they arrive on set, and then to simply get on with it without needing constant streams of praise and feedback. The director is thinking about the many technical and aesthetic aspects of the movie, not just about the actor's per-formance, so if he says nothing, we can assume he's happy. But we also need to be able to take direction: to listen, to be flexible, to respond in the moment, to take criticism on board. As in movies, so in life. We all have to work things out for ourselves and take responsibility for whatever is down to us. But at the same time you have to be open to what the guv'nor has to say—whether that means the boss, the client or your partner in life.

I have worked with at least a hundred directors in my seven decades in the movies, including some of the very best in the business. I have learnt to start out from the position of trusting that the direc-tor knows what he's doing. It might not always be obvious to me why he seems to be letting another actor get away with terribly bad acting, or why he has called, "Go again," for yet another take when I said my lines perfectly, or why he wants me to try it a different way, but that's because I can't see the big picture: I can see it only from my limited point of view. The director might be looking for something I haven't thought about; he might have seen something I haven't; or he might be intending to edit things in a way that wouldn't occur to me. All directors want what is best for the whole picture, and most of them know how to achieve that. So I try to take whatever's thrown at me and go with it.

Whether your director (or your boss) is good, bad or ugly, for the time you are stuck with them, you have to do your best to make it work. And, whether good, bad or ugly, I have learnt something from every director I have worked with. In fact, although it's much more difficult to do a good job under a bad director, it can be a valuable experience. I think of it as the actor's equivalent of an athlete training at altitude and running on sand. It's bloody hard work and you're not going to achieve a personal best, but it means that when you get to work with a good director, or run on a hard track, you're able to perform even better than before.

My favourite directors to work with are sparing in their direction and reassuring about their grip.

Joe Mankiewicz, who directed *Sleuth*, was a master at reassurance. I really needed it on that movie because I was intimidated to be working with Laurence Olivier, who was an iconic actor and an incorrigible upstager and scene-stealer. (An upstager is someone who keeps moving backwards, "upstage," so forces the other actors to turn their heads away from the camera in order to say their lines to him. A scene-stealer is someone who puts in a little raised eyebrow or twitchy nose, drawing focus to them at your key moment. You see it in life everywhere.) Olivier was also an Oscar-winning director, so I wondered how Joe was feeling.

On my first day, before the great Lord Olivier had arrived, Joe watched me walking myself quietly around the set. I must have been exuding unease because he let me finish, then came over and put his arm around my shoulders. "Don't worry, Michael," he said, "I'll take care of you." It was just what I needed to hear.

A few days later I was concerned again, though. Larry was a force of nature who conducted himself at all times at the very highest level of intensity, and he wanted to be front and centre in every scene. Larry would position himself where he wanted to be, and I was expected to act around him. Whenever a line of mine interfered with a move of his, he would order Joe to cut it. Eventually I went to Joe to complain.

"Don't worry, Michael," he said again. "I said I'd take care of you and I will. Every time I promised to cut a line, I promised to cut it in the editing. Did you notice? And the next time Larry turns you around, turn right around and I'll put a second camera over his shoulder for a close-up on you. We have skilled camera operators and an editing suite. It will all be taken care of. Trust me." I did, and it was.

I twice had the tremendous experience of being directed by the man I regarded as the greatest all-round movie talent of our time, the late great John Huston: fifteen-time Academy Award nominee, director of my childhood heroes, director of three of my all-time favourite childhood movies—*The African Queen, The Treasure of the Sierra Madre, The Maltese Falcon*. John first cast me in *The Man Who Would Be King*, in the part of Peachy Carnehan that he had originally written twenty years earlier for my idol Humphrey Bogart. We worked together a second time in *Escape to Victory* in 1981.

John was something of a father-figure to me. He was very gentle with actors because he loved being one himself, and he had an aura about him—charisma maybe, or star quality—that seemed effortlessly to command attention and respect.

It was John who taught me not to expect constant input from a director—and that the quality of a director's input could not always be measured by the number of times he interacted with me or the number of words he threw in my direction.

When we were working together on *The Man Who Would Be King* in 1975, something started to bother me and, after a few days, I brought it up. "John," I said, "you never give me any direction."

"Michael," said John, in that laconic Wild West–style voice, like gravel, or like God, "you get paid a great deal of money to do this. You don't need me to tell you what to do." He was right. After that, a director moving on to his next shot was all the indication I needed that he was happy with my performance.

In the end, though, he did give me a direction, with the minimum of words and fuss. A day or two later he anchored my character for me in just a few words. I was in the middle of a long speech and I thought it was going very well when suddenly John shouted, "Cut." He looked at me and smiled a slow smile. "You can speak faster. He's an honest man." His point, which was dead right, was that honest men don't need to take the time to think about their words or study the impact they're making. They just talk.

Lewis Gilbert directed me in *Alfie* in 1966, for which I got my first Academy Award nomination, and in *Educating Rita* in 1983, for which I earned another, so he holds a special place in my heart. He came from a similar background to me, and was an understated, sincere man with a feeling for actors. Like John Huston, he believed in letting actors get on with it unless he spotted some fatal flaw in their performance, at which point he could put you back on track with just a few words. I found him a joy to work with.

It was Lewis who made the to-camera pieces in *Alfie* work so well. Our first instinct had been to treat them like "asides" in theatre, where an actor steps away from the main action to address the audience. I spoke my lines into the camera as though I was making a long declaratory speech to a packed auditorium, basing my performance on Laurence Olivier in *Richard III* and Tom Finney in *Tom Jones*. "Cut," said Lewis. "It's not working. We need something more intimate, more current." He moved the camera in, and asked me to try it again, but this time as though I was speaking to just one close confidant. It was an unusual idea but I knew exactly who I was going to be speaking to: my friend Jim. Jim would have entirely appreciated Alfie's tastier remarks, and imagining him on the other side of the camera gave me the air of cheeky charm and supreme confidence that I needed to deliver them. That delivery somehow got the cinema audience rooting for Alfie, even if they didn't entirely approve of all of his amoral antics.

Brian De Palma was quite shy and reserved, perhaps even a little cold. By way of illustration, I did one scene for him where I wound up having hysterics in a heap on the floor. We were shooting and I was there on my own, breaking down and crying, giving it my all. Eventually Brian said, "Cut!," walked over to me lying on the floor, put his hand down to help me up and said, "Great."

"Huh," said the cameraman. "He must really like you. I've never seen him that emotional before." Brian was chilly and the movie, *Dressed to Kill*, was a bit dark for my tastes, but I enjoyed the challenge of working with such an exacting director and incredibly skilled technician. Brian would just keep shooting until he got exactly what he wanted. One shot involved a 360-degree swing of the camera and took twenty-six takes—twenty-five more than I usually like.

Mike Myers, by contrast, was warm, crazy and determined that he and everyone else should have fun. In *Austin Powers in Goldmember*, I played Nigel Powers, Austin's father. It was essentially a send-up of the sixties man-about-town—a send-up of me, or at least my image from that time—and I loved every moment. Mike, who was starring and directing, is as wacky in real life as he seems in his movies and liked to play rock 'n' roll between takes. At first I didn't take to having this music blasting out when I was trying to remember my lines. But I got used to it, and then I started looking forward to it. A couple of times we even had a little dance. Mike loves what he does and he makes sure everyone else has a blast too.

The director for whom I have made the most movies, and perhaps the director with whom I have felt most comfortable in my entire career, is Christopher Nolan, a brilliant London-born writer-director whom I consider to be the David Lean of his generation. I have had the enormous privilege of appearing in seven of Chris's movies: his three blockbuster *Batman* movies, his three super-clever mind-bender movies, *The Prestige, Interstellar* and *Inception* and, most recently, the terrific *Dunkirk*. Chris calls me his lucky charm: when there was no part for me in *Dunkirk*, he cast me as the voice of the squadron leader who talks to the pilots over their radios, to make sure I was there in the credits. I feel that it's more the other way: he is *my* lucky charm. Chris Nolan is a fabulously clever writer and director and some of his movies that I have acted in I still don't fully understand. (Chris did reveal to me that the only bits of *Inception* that are real, as opposed to dreams or imagination, are the bits I'm in. Still, when people ask me what it's about, I just say, "It's about two hours.")

In his directorial style he reminds me very much of that other great writer-director John Huston. Like John, he is sparing and softly spoken but always on-the-nose with his direction. If he needs you to alter something, he won't shout, "Cut." He will let you go through the whole take, then wander over and tell you, in a very gentle and understated way, after a sip from the flask of tea he keeps going at all times "Can we do another one, Michael? And this time could you do it this way?" It's all very calm. There is never a raised voice. He is the exemplar of quiet authority. To be honest, if you walked onto the set you wouldn't even know who the director was because he's just wandering around, no ego, very quiet.

And, like John, he can be this way because he has put the effort in up front. He has a crystal-clear vision, terrific scripts with real characters, a great producer, Emma Thomas, who also happens to be his wife, and he casts like a dream. I remember I once asked John what the art of direction was. "Casting," he replied. "If you cast it right, you don't have to tell the actors what to do." Chris Nolan is the same. I don't want to sound conceited but his casting is wonderful.

I remember, for example, the first scene I made on my first Chris Nolan movie, *Batman Begins*, in 2005. It was with Christian Bale, the best Batman ever in my view. Great casting. And after just the second take, Chris said, "Cut, print," and we were off.

Chris brought Christian Bale and me together again the following year for *The Prestige*, a story about magicians, violence and love, this time joined by Hugh Jackman, who is one of my favourite actors and people. Hugh can do everything: sing, dance and act in the cinema and the theatre, and he is terrific to work with too. To top it all I was working with two brilliant and beautiful actresses, Scarlett Johansson and Rebecca Hall, and with David Bowie like you've never seen him before, very strait-laced and severe, looking like a middle-aged banker in a suit and tie and moustache.

In 2010 Chris pulled together another stunning cast for *Inception*: Leonardo DiCaprio, Tom Hardy, Ellen Page, Cillian Murphy, Joseph Gordon-Levitt, Marion Cotillard and Ken Watanabe. And in 2014 he did it again with *Interstellar*, whose cast included Jessica Chastain, Anne Hathaway, Ellen Burstyn, Matthew McConaughey and Casey Affleck. Between the six of us we have six Academy Awards and twenty nominations—and I'm sure more to come.

And Chris not only casts wonderful actors, he also re-casts them. I am not the only one he has used again and again in his movies. In fact, he has almost created his own little repertory company.

My point is that, in my experience, the best directors, like the best leaders in other industries, achieve great things by gathering the right people around them, then trusting them to get on with what they do best, giving them a quiet nudge whenever they need it to keep them on track. That approach tends to make everyone—actors and crew—do their best work: happy, productive and tremendously loyal.

👓 *The bad and the ugly*

Bad directors are bad for all the same reasons other bosses are bad. They are not good enough at their jobs, they don't work hard enough, or they are bullies.

Of course it's more fun to learn from good directors. But even the bad ones have things to teach you. Like self-protection and self-reliance, which are part of being a true professional. And in the very worst cases they might force you to learn how to direct yourself. There was one movie I worked on where it quickly became clear to the entire cast that the director was off with the fairies, probably tapping them up for the fairy dust he seemed to have developed a taste for. We realised we'd have to deliver the picture ourselves. (We did, and the director in question was deemed to have done a fabulous job. The boss takes credit for other people's work in all walks of life.)

On another occasion, a movie with a stellar cast working at the top of their game was ruined by an illustrious veteran director, who one day openly admitted to me that he was only still directing to fund his very expensive hobby of deep-sea fishing off the coast of California. As soon as the filming was done and he had been paid, off he went. He was at sea and, sadly, so were editing and post-production without him.

The hardest directors to work with—and unfortunately you find them in every workplace, every family, every community of people—are the bullies. My approach with bullies has always been to make it clear from the start that I won't be their victim. When I worked with Otto Preminger on *Hurry Sundown* in 1966, I knew his reputation as a monstrous tyrant who was happiest when everyone else was miserable. I had heard that he liked to scream at actors and crew alike. So the first day I met him, I told him, "You need to know, Otto, that I'm very sensitive. You mustn't shout at me. If anyone shouts at me when I'm working I burst into tears and I can't work for the rest of the day." Otto stared back at me. He seemed genuinely puzzled. Or perhaps, I thought, he was getting ready for a particularly big scream.

"But why do you think I would do that?" he finally asked.

"Well," I said—I stayed calm, "I have friends who worked with you on *Saint Joan* and they said you shouted."

"You shouldn't make such friends," said Otto. "I only shout at bad actors. And I would never shout at Alfie."

Whether because he considered me a good actor, because he loved Alfie, or, more likely, because I had made things clear at the start, Otto never shouted at me. He did, though, give everyone else a terrible time, especially my young co-star Faye Dunaway. My little talk hadn't managed to change his personality, only to protect me personally from it. Otto tormented the inexperienced and sweet Faye, who ended up in tears most days. Of course everyone worked in a state of abject terror, which was not only deeply unpleasant, but also did nothing for the quality of the movie, since no one can give their best when they are frigid with fear of doing something wrong and being screamed at. And Faye ended up paying a lot of money to get out of her six-movie contract with Otto, going on to become an enormous star.

Disagreeing with a good director is very different from having to work with a bad one. I adopt a couple of approaches in this situation. If I am convinced the direction I want to take with a particular scene is the right one, I may suggest a compromise. I may propose we try it his way, and try it my way, and then he can decide when he sees the rushes. The director usually agrees—and usually turns out to be right. I've got my point of view, but he has the vision and is seeing the bigger picture. But at least this way I get the chance to see I'm wrong. Then again, sometimes I just tell the director he's right, then go my own way anyway. What I never do is have a stand-up row about it.

ᎶᏅ *Take my advice…*

Part of the skill of taking direction is knowing who to listen to, and when, and who to ignore. Unfortunately an awful lot of advice is not worth hearing. People will give you advice at the drop of a hat: people who don't really know you, people who don't really know what they're talking about, people who are really giving themselves advice, not addressing you or your problems. Not to mention the critics. The best and most thoughtful critics will sometimes say some helpful things, but so many of them are so wrong so much of the time that on the whole I would advise taking criticism from your trusted circle, and from yourself—I am my own most severe critic— and ignoring the rest.

Most of the advice I received in the first thirty years of my life can be very quickly summarised: "Give up." So I formed a habit of ignoring any advice that came my way and following my own path. That worked out fine, as it happens, but I've changed that habit now. Now I would recommend searching out a small group of people—mine is made up mainly of agents, close friends, my wife and, of course, a very good accountant—who know you well, who know what you want, who have your interests at heart and who know more than you do. Listen to them. Look to them for advice and direction. Tune out everyone else—especially the critics.

A good agent will guide, protect, advocate and champion. Most of us have these people in our lives, even if we don't give them the professional title of agent and 10 per cent of our earnings. Choose your agent well: they can have a profound impact on your career.

My first, Jimmy Fraser, had impressive offices on Regent Street. I was too small a fish for him, he never seemed hugely keen on me and he dropped me as soon as he saw the finished film of *A Hill in Korea*, telling me I would never get anywhere. Sound familiar? I heard it a lot. Mind you, Jimmy did get me that film in the first place so I have to thank him for that. And he was right: I was terrible in it.

My next was the wonderful and dogged Josephine Burton. Josephine was one of the first professionals who ever believed in me. But she struggled to find me work (this was the era of Joan Littlewood and endless small TV and theatre roles). When she died unexpectedly, and much too young, during a routine operation, it was an immense personal and professional blow.

It was another couple of years before I struck agent gold. I had written to Dennis Selinger, the top actors' agent in the UK, asking him to take me on, but he had declined. Then, in 1961, he saw me in *The Compartment* and changed his mind. It was a key moment in my career. Dennis was the perfect agent. He had wonderful contacts and wonderful judgement. He was kind and gentle, not a shouter and screamer. He was very commercial but he was not greedy. And he was savvy and far-sighted enough to know that at that point I needed critical as well as commercial success: I had to appear in the right shows, and come to the attention of influential people, not just do whatever would make the most money.

Later, when I made my first real money, four thousand pounds, on *Zulu*, and promptly burned my way straight through it, it was Dennis who persuaded me to open a bank account (which consisted of a thousand-pound overdraft) and get an accountant. It was Dennis who flew out to Las Vegas to give Shakira away when we got married in 1973. The night my daughter Natasha was born, I went straight from the hospital to Dennis's house to tell him the good news. Over the following two weeks, when she became dangerously ill, I stayed with Dennis, who was a tower of strength. He became my closest friend and most valued mentor. He died in 1998 and I miss him still.

Dennis was UK-based, and when I arrived in Hollywood I needed a local guide. I was immensely fortunate to end up as the least-known client of the fierce and fiercely loyal Sue Mengers, Hollywood's most powerful agent at the time. Sue held extraordinary and much sought-after get-togethers in Hollywood. It was usually meatloaf on the menu, and she always instructed us to be out of her house by ten thirty. The fun was seeing who else would be there because Sue cast her dinners like she would cast a movie: the night we turned up and found Barbra Streisand, Sting and Sheryl Crow around the table was not unusual. Another memorable night featured Princess Margaret, Jack Nicholson, Clint Eastwood and, by special request, Barry Manilow. Sue loved her food almost as much as she loved her clients, and after her death Bette Midler starred in a one-woman show about her called *I'll Eat You Last: A Chat with Sue Mengers*. When I went to see it, I

enjoyed every moment but one. At that point Bette
Midler answers the phone, sighs, turns to the audience and puts the phone down again. She says,
"Michael Caine just left me." An audience of six
hundred people turned and looked at me with utter malice. It's true, I did leave Sue once. I can't
remember why. Anyway, I soon realised my mistake
because my new agent got me a role in Steven Sea-
gal's *On Deadly Ground*, shooting in Alaska. I made
it up with Sue and went back to her.

Dennis was irreplaceable and Sue was a unique
human being, but I landed on my feet again.

When she retired Sue Mengers strongly approved
of my move to the passionate, driven and determined Toni Howard, another giant of the Hollywood scene. Toni has believed in me, loved me and
protected me for well over twenty years now. Since
1994 she has guided my career beautifully and she
is now the one person I listen to when I'm making big decisions. She is a dear friend too, almost
family, in fact. Shakira and I think of Toni, her
husband David, her sister Wendy and Wendy's husband Leonard as our Hollywood family. Meanwhile,
my agents in England, for the last few years the
wonderful Kate Buckley-Sharma, have found me
amazing British projects that I was able to do without leaving home.

An actor also needs a talented and loyal press

agent, a ruthless lawyer and a wise business manager. I have been fortunate enough to have all of
these. Like a director whose secret ingredient is
casting, I sometimes think my secret ingredient is
the people I choose to put around me.

I couldn't end this chapter without mentioning
the friends who have stayed with me through thick
and thin, often offering great advice at just the
right moment. Shakira and I have a wonderfully
supportive group of friends, from within the industry and outside it: friends to have dinner with,
and friends, like Dorrit Moussaieff, married to the
former President of Iceland Ólafur Grímsson and
Natasha's godmother, who we know we could call
in the middle of the night and she would be there
for us. But if I could pick out one, then the one
friend whose advice changed the course of my life
was Jack Nicholson. Not everyone's idea of a fairy
godmother, I grant you, but for me, Jack will always be holding a magic wand and wearing a tiara.
He persuaded me to come out of my first retirement
and, in *Blood and Wine*, he also gave me the vehicle
to do it with. It was a turning point in my career
when I was down and almost out. But that's for another chapter.

10.

The Big Picture

"It's a very difficult job and the only way to get through it is we all work together as a team. And that means you do everything I say."

The Italian Job, 1969

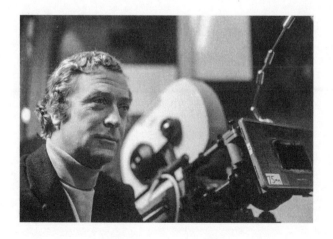

THE AWARD-CEREMONY SPEECH in which the big star thanks a great long list of people "without whom none of this would have been possible" is by now a cliché. But making a movie really is a tremendous team effort: the makeup artists, the set designers, the caterers, the sound engineers, the lighting technicians, the camera operators, the producers. The list goes on and on. Everyone has a role to play. Everyone is as much of an expert in what they do as you are in what you do. No one is more important than anyone else. And everyone is focused on the same thing: making the best movie possible.

In every movie, I think of the whole team as my temporary family and my route to success, so I don't ever put myself above anyone else, and I don't put myself in competition with the other actors. Instead, I try to understand what other people in the team can do for me, and what I can do for them, to help everyone make a better movie.

And it's not just movies. It was the same for me in

the restaurant business, and I bet it's the same in any other enterprise. I might have been the owner but it takes the whole team—every chef, every waiter, every cleaner and washer-upper—doing their jobs and doing their best to send the customers away happy at the end of their dinners.

👓 *Don't put yourself above anyone else*

When you're referred to as "the talent" and when you arrive on set in a chauffeur-driven limousine, only to become the prime focus of a swarm of charming hair and makeup artists, and when electricians are scrambling up on scaffolding to re-set the light so there is a lovely glint in your eye, it's easy to start to believe the hype. Don't. Yes, everyone is trying their best to make you feel happy and relaxed. Yes, everyone is focused on helping you to look and sound your best. But that is not because you are more important than they are. It is because they want to get the best performance possible out of you, for the good of the team. Try to remember that the runner holding an umbrella when you take a walk in the rain is there for the costume, not for you.

I try to establish friendly and relaxed relations with everyone from the moment I walk on to the set. It's the right thing to do, and it makes everything go better, for the movie and for me. If the crew are feeling fabulous they will do their jobs better. If you are good to everyone on the unit, chances are they will be good to you. Anyway, if you try to work out who is "important" and who is not, and treat them accordingly, you'll be caught out by your own prejudices.

John Huston was a strapping great man's man, and his writing partner was a little old lady called Gladys Hill. She looked like a secretary but she was actually very influential. It would have been easy to overlook her, but it would have been wrong. I find it easier just to treat everyone the same. At least until they give me reason to do otherwise.

👓 *What can I do for you?*

To understand what other members of the team can do for me, and what I can do to make their lives easier, it helps if I understand the whole process of film-making, not just my little part of it: the commercial process and the creative process, the financial and the technical.

In any walk of life it will usually be worthwhile to take the time to understand where others are coming from and what their priorities and requirements are.

Understanding the process, I've found, can be much more important than understanding the piece itself. I can't tell you how many plays and movies I have appeared in that I didn't fully understand, from *R.U.R.,* the obscure Karel Čapek play in which fourteen-year-old me made his debut as a robot, to Chris Nolan's *Inception* and *Interstellar*, via everything by Harold Pinter: I appeared in his first play *The Room* and his last work, a re-make of *Sleuth*.

But what I always keep in mind as a basic commercial consideration is that anything an actor does that introduces delay is going to cost the production time and money—and probably you your next job. So, as you probably know by now, prepare yourself well and turn up on time are my first rules in life.

It is also crucially important that actors understand the technical requirements of the camera operators, the sound engineers, the lighting technicians, the continuity folk and so on, so that they can prepare their own contribution with those in mind. For example, it's no good thinking up some complicated physical mannerism if you're not going to be able to repeat it exactly, shot after shot, possibly over several days. In movie-making you will usually need to repeat any sequence at least three times: once for the long shot or master shot, once for the medium shot and once for the close-up. If you fiddle around in the long shot you will have to be able to repeat that fiddle exactly in every shot—or the long shot will have to be shot again. For the sake of the continuity folk, I keep my mannerisms and actions simple, precise, planned and logical, so that I can execute them effortlessly and accurately again and again. You can think of the continuity folk as terrible fusspots or, as I prefer to, as your indispensable best friends on set. You can't do the second take without them.

Camera operators are less fussy. You'd be surprised by the places I've seen cameras put when really necessary. It's useful to know this. It means that when I'm rehearsing I'll move to wherever seems right for me, and wait to be told if that is going to cause a problem. Of course, sometimes the director says, "I don't want a discussion about it. You need to end up exactly there." And then I do. There are also various things you can do to help the camera operator help you. If the director tells me to run from right over there, towards the camera and then past it, I run like hell when I'm far away, then slow down as I approach the camera. Otherwise I go by too fast and I'm just a blur. I learnt that from James Cagney. And if I'm sitting down for a close-up and have to stand, I do that slowly too, and on cue, to give the camera the chance to follow me. In close-up, any sudden movements and I'm out of the frame.

Sound technicians are never happy so their unhappiness can to some extent be discounted. However, if you want to avoid a boom being "accidentally" dropped on your head, make sure the sound technician knows in advance when you're planning on switching from a whisper to a roar. In one of the many features in which I played some kind of gangster in the early stages of my career, I was supposed to creep up to a guy, whisper, "Time's up," and shoot him in the back. The sound technician, listening through his big headphones, had his equipment turned up to full volume so he could hear the whisper, and was all set to turn it back down low for the shot. I did my walk, then forgot to say the line and just fired the shot. The sound engineer took the rest of the day off.

Since we actors very much want to stay alive, I also make a point of understanding a little bit about the world of stunt artists, so I'm not afraid to draw the line. Sometimes we all have to be our own health and safety officer.

If you look at it from other people's point of view it will become clear why you should never do a dangerous stunt on the last day of a picture. The change in attitude to your personal well-being is a bit like the change you encounter from a salesperson before and after you sign that piece of paper, or from a company that has been trying to woo you before and after you accept their job offer.

I learnt this from Stanley Baker, the producer of *Zulu*. It was not the last day of the movie but the second, but a similar principle applied. You may remember from an earlier chapter that on those first days of shooting my horse and I did not see eye to eye and I spent a great deal of time lying on the ground, or in water, in the various undignified positions into which my horse had thrown me. I was a bit aggrieved that no one seemed bothered about my back at the end of the first day's filming, or my knees at the end of the second. Everyone seemed concerned about the horse, the sun, even my costume— was it ripped? Was it dirty?—but not a word about whether I was OK. I brought it up with Stanley Baker and he explained, with a grin. "Simple," he said. "You've only done two scenes and at this point we could easily replace you—probably more cheaply than we could replace the horse." I opened my mouth to protest but he went on, "The more shots you're in, the more careful we'll be about you. Towards the end you will become extremely precious to us and we will overwhelm you with fuss, care and attention. Until the final scene, when, once again, we won't give a shit. Golden rule, Michael: never do a dangerous stunt on the last day of a picture." And I never have. In fact, I prefer to leave the stunts to the stunt artists. I don't want to do them out of their jobs, and I don't want to do myself out of a limb.

Billion Dollar Brain, my third Harry Palmer movie, was shot on location in Finland, a beautiful and inconceivably cold country where we spent days filming on the melting ice floes, hoping they wouldn't crack and, meanwhile, standing in three inches of melting ice water. At one point the director, Ken Russell, was asking me to jump into a hole in the ice. It's the kind of thing Harry might do but it wasn't the kind of thing I much fancied doing. I had a Finnish stand-in, though, and I thought he probably wouldn't mind. I wandered up to him and said, "How would you like to earn a bit of extra money? Could you just warm up in the sauna and then jump into that hole in the ice?"

He gave me a long look. "What?"

"You know, jump in the ice. Like Finnish people do."

"No, we don't. We would have heart attacks."

Neither of us jumped into the ice.

Stunt artists save our lives—literally. Editors do it metaphorically. Skilled editing can make an enormous difference to a performance, finessing poor timing and removing awkward movements. A cut to a great reaction shot can make a bungled line seem much stronger than it actually was. But, of course, an editor can also cut you out entirely and kill your performance completely.

Sometimes an editor will "kill your darling" or

edit out your favourite moment. It's painful but they're generally right. It happened to me on *Without a Clue*, the 1980s movie in which I played Sherlock Holmes. When I saw the edited version of the sword fight at the end of the movie I said to the editor, "You cut the funniest moment in the entire film—the slow reaction I did at the end."

"I know exactly the look you're talking about," said the editor. "It would have been very funny. But the reaction took five seconds and at this point in the movie we need pace. Look, this is what it would look like with your reaction in there." He fiddled about for a minute, then ran it back for me, and I saw he was right. Careers are made and broken by editors, and funny moments are killed, but you can be sure that they'll be doing what is best for the film as a whole.

In a movie (and, by the way, it's a completely different story in the theatre—which emphasises how important it is to understand the industry you're in and the precise way it works), the people whose performances I'm least concerned about are those of other actors. At least, I try not to be concerned. I have to admit that the one thing that can steal my focus on set is terrible acting. It fascinates me and distracts me. But it isn't my concern. If another actor isn't giving me what I want, I try to act as though he is. I try to put in my own best possible performance and act and react as if I'm getting the ideal performance back. I try to trust that the director has a plan and will make it right: perhaps the other actor will end up on the cutting-room floor. Critiquing my colleagues or interfering with their performances does not count as teamwork.

That is, unless they're deliberately trying to undermine my performance, or the movie itself. There are attention-seekers, limelight-hoggers, deceivers and bullies in every office and every family, and the film set is certainly no exception. Generally the director will pick up on this and deal with it himself. If he doesn't, I find a long stare before I say my next line generally does the trick.

The flip side of trying to ignore bad acting is trying not to get concerned about whether the other fellow in a scene is "out-acting" me. It should never be about trying to make myself appear better than the other guy, because everything must be done for the good of the whole. That's why I'm not one of those actors who eases up on my performance when I'm "off-camera" feeding lines for someone else's close-up. Maybe I'm not the one in the spotlight but I still have a contribution to make so that the scene is the best it can be. Whether I'm on-camera or off-camera, whether it is my close-up or I'm just feeding lines, I play my role at the same pitch and with the same energy. A real team player understands that part of their contribution is doing whatever it takes to ensure everyone is giving their best.

And, of course, a generous double-act can be greater than the sum of its parts. I discovered that when I played Peachy, opposite Sean Connery as Danny, in *The Man Who Would Be King.* We each understood that, for the sake of the picture, we had to bring each other into our close-ups rather than edging each other out. In long dialogue scenes, Sean would turn me full face to the camera for my important line, and I would return the compliment. Sean is one of the most unselfish actors I have ever worked with and we developed a deep mutual trust and admiration. We were always thinking of each other, and the film was all the better for it. However full of stars a team is—a movie team, a football team—if those stars are too full of their own importance to work as a team, they are going to get beaten by a weaker side that has learnt to work together.

👓 *Only compete with yourself*

Montgomery Clift used to say that the highest tribute you could pay to another actor was to envy his performance. He thought it was healthy for one actor to look at another and think, I wish that had been me. I disagree. This kind of competitive comparison is rarely even possible, and when it is, it is pointless and unhelpful.

I love to go to the theatre and the movies, and I love watching TV. I absolutely love other actors, their skills and performances. I admire them and get great pleasure out of watching what they do. But I have no sense of competition with other actors—my predecessors, my contemporaries or my successors. I love Humphrey Bogart, I love Marlon Brando. They are my heroes, my idols. But I'd never put myself up against them, and it's of no interest to me whether I'm as good as them or not. There's just no point in doing that, no possible advantage. I'm as good as I am, which is the best I can do.

My competition is always with myself. From my very first step on stage as a robot for Clubland to my latest movie role, all I ever do is try to be the best I can possibly be, without reference to being better than anyone else. How can I find a role that stretches me further? How can I make this role better than the last role? How can I make this film better than the last film? How can I make this take better than the last take?

What makes my heart sing is not besting another actor but besting myself. The roles of which I am proudest are the ones that have asked the most of me, that have been the furthest away from me, but that I feel I have made the most real. The parts where I feel I have truly managed to make myself disappear and summon up someone else: Frank, the disillusioned alcoholic university professor in *Educating Rita*; Dr. Larch, the rule-stretching gynaecologist addicted to ether in *The Cider House Rules*; Thomas Fowler, the foreign correspondent in *The Quiet American*; Alfred Penny-worth, the wise and patient butler who knows how to handle himself in Chris Nolan's *Batman* movies; Ray Say, the seedy, angry and desperate agent in *Little Voice*; Harry Brown, the pensioner who loses his rag and goes on a rampage in *Harry Brown*; Fred Ballinger, the fading retired composer in *Youth*; and, of course, Alfie.

The only time it is useful for me to decide how talented another actor is, is when I'm considering working with him, or when I'm already working with him and trying to learn from him. Because I only want to work with the best and I only want to learn from the best. Other than that, it's of no interest.

I tell my grandchildren the same thing. There will always be someone faster than you, cleverer than you, better-looking than you, richer than you, luckier than you. So forget competing with other people: it will just make you bitter, self-pitying, unhappy.

Do your own thing, and do it as well as you possibly can.

When I was young, I read something urging Olympic athletes to "chase the dream, not the competition." That line has stayed with me all my professional life. It is sound advice.

PART THREE

The Long Run

11.

Being a Star (or Why I Never Wear Suede Shoes)

Ray Say: "You're a star."
LV: "You're a nutter."

Little Voice, 1998

GETTING TO THE TOP—to where you wanted to be—is a bit like climbing up a steep mountain path, reaching the peak, then taking in the view. It's bloody fantastic. Perhaps it's even better than you'd been anticipating. But it can also be a bit disorienting. Alongside the overwhelming feelings of achievement and elation, there is sometimes another feeling, peering down over the edge, of slight nausea. Standing at the summit does not always feel quite how you expected it would when you were looking at it from halfway up.

So what *can* you expect, if you become a star in the movies, or any other universe?

Let's start with the good bits. One of the most exciting things that happened to me when I became a star was I got to mix with other stars, which meant I got to meet my heroes. Someone said, "Don't meet your heroes because you'll be disappointed," but I disagree. Getting to meet my heroes, and in many cases become friends with them, was, for me, one of the best parts of becoming a star.

It all happened very fast. After the success of *Alfie*, Shirley MacLaine chose me to play opposite her in *Gambit*, which was to be shot in Hollywood, the centre of the movie universe. I flew out to Los Angeles and was whisked off in a Rolls-Royce to a luxury suite at the Beverly Hills Hotel on Sunset Boulevard, where I was to stay for the entire three-month shoot. While I was waiting for Shirley, who was delayed for a few days, I hung out in the gorgeous airy lobby spotting stars and, to my great pleasure, being spotted right back. Jane Russell, one of Hollywood's biggest and sexiest stars of the 1940s and 1950s, invited me to lunch at the Beverly Wilshire. John "call me Duke" Wayne landed his helicopter in the hotel's gardens before striding into the lobby in full cowboy get-up, telling me I was going to be a star and giving me the advice I opened this book with. "And never wear suede shoes," he added.

"Why not?" I asked.

"Because," he said, low and slow, "I was taking a piss the other day and the guy in the next stall recognised me and turned towards me. He said, 'John Wayne—you're my favourite actor,' and pissed all over my suede shoes."

As if that wasn't enough, when Shirley arrived back in Hollywood, this powerful and beloved Hollywood figure pulled out all the stops and threw me the most dazzling and glamorous welcome-to-

BLOWING THE BLOODY DOORS OFF

LA party. There I met icons like Gloria Swanson, Frank Sinatra and Liza Minnelli, and soon-to-be best friends, like Sidney Poitier—with whom I went on to make two movies—and the Hollywood super-agent and super-host Irving "Swifty" Lazar, so-named because he once put together three movie deals for Humphrey Bogart in a single day. The following night Shirley took me to dinner in Danny Kaye's kitchen, where the other guests were the Duke of Edinburgh and Cary Grant, and the night after that it was just a quiet family dinner—except that her quiet family dinners consisted of her mum, her dad and her brother, Warren Beatty.

At another party, thrown for me in New York, I met the legendary Bette Davis. "You remind me of the young Leslie Howard," she told me, in that unmistakable drawl. I was slim and blond at the time (I had been following the Actor's Diet, or as we called it, starving, for years) and had been told that before, but Bette's follow-up was entirely original. "Do you know?" she went on. "Leslie screwed every single woman in every movie he ever made—except me."

"Oh, yes," I spluttered. "I'd heard that."

"Well, I wasn't interested in being just another one of his conquests, and I told him so. But when I look at you, I just wonder what difference it would have made if I had." This last bit was said a little wistfully.

"Would you like dinner tonight?" I blurted out.

She gave me a long look, then said dismissively, "I wasn't making a pass at you."

I hadn't thought she was. I straightened things out and we had a lovely dinner that night, along with Jessica Tandy and Hume Cronyn, after which I put Bette in a taxi home.

Soon I was dating women like Natalie Wood and Nancy Sinatra. I was being flown out for my first visit to Las Vegas by that city's king, Nancy's father Frank, to hear Frank sing with Count Basie and be introduced to the Rat Pack—Dean Martin, Sammy Davis Jr., Joey Bishop and Peter Lawford. At the beginning this was all rather surreal and overwhelming. I remember sitting in Frank's private plane, just me alone with Frank because all the women were sitting in a separate little group, and being so nervous I could barely speak. Later it became normal for me to socialise with Gregory Peck, Frank Sinatra, Mia Farrow, Billy Wilder, Jack Nicholson. They were simply my friends. But I never lost a sense of wonder and gratitude each time I came across a movie hero.

One star-studded dinner that stands out in my memory for the sheer incredulity it prompted took place not in Hollywood but in glamorous Budapest. I was shooting a movie there and so, it seemed, was everyone else. Elizabeth Taylor threw a birthday party one night and there came a point in the evening when all the other men at my table must have gone to the Gents because I remember looking around me and it was just me, sitting at a table with my wife Shakira, Elizabeth, Raquel Welch and Grace Kelly.

Two of the most star-studded events of my life must have been my sixtieth and eightieth birthday parties, both shared with my "celestial twin" (we were born at the same time on the same day, me in London and him in Chicago), Quincy Jones.

For our sixtieth birthdays in 1993 we took over a club on Beverly Drive and it was wonderful to see so many family and friends from past and present all gathered together—from John Barry and Sidney Furie of my *Ipcress File* days to Oprah Winfrey and Jack Nicholson. The highlight of the night was rapping with Ice-T. I thought I was actually pretty good.

Our eightieth birthday party had to top that— and it did. How do you top a birthday party in Los Angeles? You head to Las Vegas and the dining room of the MGM Grand. There were two thousand guests; the cabaret included Stevie Wonder singing "Happy Birthday," Jennifer Hudson, Whoopi Goldberg, Bono and Chaka Khan; my wife, daughters and closest friends were there; and we raised millions of dollars for the Lou Ruvo Center for

Brain Health, founded by my friend Larry in honour of his father and specialising in looking after people suffering from Alzheimer's and Parkinson's. It was a wonderful, joyful evening, and looking around me as Chaka Khan sang the theme tune from *Alfie* to me, I thought, That's what it's all about.

Stardom also brought me life-changing quantities of money. I don't have a lot of good advice on money. I'm good at earning it, but I'm terrible at hanging on to it. I suppose what I would say is: spend it on what gives you pleasure. When I made my first real money, on *Zulu*, I spent it on a pony for my horse-mad eight-year-old daughter Dominique. When I first felt truly wealthy, after *Ipcress*, I went mad buying things I had never been able to afford. It might sound silly but it turned out that my first priority wasn't a fancy car or a foreign holiday, but hygiene. When you're really poor, you're often dirty as well. I had been used to making shirts last another day, brushing my teeth with salt, doing without shampoo and sleeping in unwashed bedclothes because I had no money for the launderette. So I went mad buying shirts, sheets, towels, socks, toothpaste, shampoo and the world's biggest collection of aftershave. As the money kept coming in, I bought a house for my mum, two houses for my brother and a flat for my friend Paul. I also eventually managed to persuade Mum to give up her cleaning jobs. My family had never had much money to speak of and it gave me enormous pleasure to be able to make them more comfortable. Now I've stopped buying houses and I spend my money on huge family holidays, with all the grandchildren. But no matter how much money I make, I never lose that feeling of panic and dread at the thought of being poor again. I never feel completely secure. I think when you've been really poor, that feeling goes deep and never leaves.

The only other piece of money advice I have that's worth sharing is something David Bowie once told me. I was with him on the day he bought himself a yacht. He took me on board and we had a drink. I met him a couple of years later and asked how he was enjoying it. "There are two great things about a yacht, Michael," he said. "The day you buy it, and the day you sell it. And the last one's better than the first. Forget it, Michael, forget yachts." So I did. If I had that kind of money I wouldn't have a yacht, I'd have a plane. For me that would be the height of luxury.

Stardom opened other doors too: to the things that money can't buy. Anywhere that was impossible to get into, suddenly I could. Theatres that saved seats until the last minute for famous people saved them for me. Exclusive clubs offered me membership. Restaurants that were booked up months in advance kept their best tables for me. In New York, it was Elaine's, the city's salon where writers, directors and actors gather. In Los Angeles it was Ma Maison, Matsuhisa (the first of Nobu Matsuhisa's restaurants) and Chasen's (where I once did the Heimlich manoeuvre on George Burns and saved his life. He must have been ninety then, so he had another ten good years left in him. Never a dull moment in Chasen's.) In London it was the Aretusa on the King's Road and the White Elephant Club on Curzon Street in the 1960s, and then my own restaurant, Langan's Brasserie, and the River Café, Harry's Bar, Scott's and Annabel's.

The unexpected perks were things like this. When I first became a star I had never learnt to drive so I hired a chauffeur to drive me around. But later I moved with my family to Los Angeles, and everybody drives there so I had to take a test. Before I took it, a man behind a desk informed me, in a prepared speech he had probably given many times, "The person who will perform your test is sitting outside in the car. You will speak to him only to say, 'Good morning.' There will be no normal conversation. He will give you instructions, you will listen and respond. There will be no personal remarks whatsoever."

I said, "Yes, Officer, I understand." I went outside and got into the car.

The guy looked at me and he said, "I loved you in *The Man Who Would Be King.* You're going to have to be shit to not pass this test." So at the age of fifty that was how I got my first driver's licence.

Alongside all of this fun, glamour and privilege, there are of course some downsides to being a star, in the movies or anywhere else. But if I ever even start to feel sorry for myself about some trapping of stardom I give myself a sharp talking-to. "Michael, would you prefer the alternative?" Yes, being at the top brings its challenges. But if you think it's lonely or tough up there, either you've never been at the bottom, or you've forgotten what it was like.

One big downside of stardom is that while you're meeting your heroes and enjoying your money and all the other trappings—my first dressing room in Hollywood was bigger and more comfortable than anywhere I had lived up to that point in my life—it is easy to enter a bit of a bubble and lose touch with reality, your values and who you are. It's more for others to say than for me, but I don't think I ever really got stuck in that bubble. Perhaps that was because success came to me relatively late.

I'm sure the people I kept around me helped too. Although my social circle did become quite starry, I also continued to spend a lot of time with my family. And I never was much of one for an entourage. These days, we have security, a housekeeper and a brilliant secretary: that's about the extent of it. I've never had bodyguards, cooks, personal trainers or stylists. If I'm doing press, I won't be surrounded by PR, agents or assistants. Shakira and I love seeing small groups of friends, and we love spending time with our family, but we don't like to have lots of staff around and we are really quite self-sufficient.

This doesn't just go for those of us in the position to have "people," it goes for any senior manager in any organisation: the more people there are around you, whose job it is to please you, or whose job depends on winding you up and getting you exercised about this or that, or whose sense of importance depends on their relationship with you, the more likely you are to lose touch with reality. Not to mention the more sinister possibility of exploitation and manipulation by people whose livelihoods are built around your success.

I remember one night I introduced Whitney Houston at a charity show in Hollywood. She was with me backstage and before she went on someone who I assumed was a member of her entourage came up to her, put her up against the back of the stage, put her arms either side of her so she was pinned there, then talked right into her face. "You're going to do this, and do that, you've got to, you've got to," on and on and on. I walked on stage and said, "Ladies and gentlemen, Whitney Houston," and she let Whitney go, and on Whitney walked. And she was fabulous. But I felt for her.

Another downside of being a star: you can get in everywhere, but you can't get out anywhere. Or not without a circus of press and fans accompanying you. This point was first brought home to me in 1967 when *The Ipcress File* was shown at the Cannes Film Festival and I was put up in a very grand suite at the Carlton Hotel. It was undreamt-of glamour and luxury for me. Which was lucky, because it was difficult for me to leave my suite without being mobbed by the press. These days, everyone has a camera on them and everyone wants a selfie.

But I don't get upset about it. I enjoy it, and I remind myself that it's better than the alternative. Some truly great stars are content to remain behind their on-screen personas.

Once I was waiting outside the Beverly Hills Hotel with Cary Grant. We had bumped into each other and were just chatting when a tourist noticed us and rushed over. "Michael Caine," she said breathlessly, "is it really you? I've been in Hollywood for two weeks and you're the first movie star I've seen." She turned to Cary Grant. "You just never see movie stars in Hollywood, do you?"

"No, ma'am," answered Cary, politely. "You don't." Cary didn't mind a bit, though.

But when I had a similar experience, I felt differently. I was shooting *The Wilby Conspiracy*, an anti-apartheid movie, with Sidney Poitier, in Kenya in the mid-1970s. Sidney was a massive star in Hollywood but in Kenya he was treated like a god. Meanwhile I was completely safe to break out my suede shoes: no one in Kenya seemed to know or care who I was. Even the man sent to meet Shakira, baby Natasha and me at the airport had no idea who I was. It was a strange sensation after years of fame, and although I tried to enjoy being able to walk down the street without being harassed by fans, the novelty soon wore off. I realised I had actually come to get a kick out of the recognition.

Other stars claim not to enjoy the attention. I was in Capri with Elton John a few years ago and we were walking up Via Camerelle, the island's beautiful main shopping street, full of boutiques and designer stores. Elton stopped at a watch shop and we were soon joined by a swarm of paparazzi and fans. He started to grumble to me about always being recognised and bothered by photographers. I love Elton dearly, and I admire his dress sense, but I suggested that life would have been easier that day if he had chosen a different outfit. I was in my usual dark blue slacks and black T-shirt with sunglasses and a baseball cap. Elton was dressed in a bright yellow suit and a ton of bling.

As Frank Sinatra said to me when I was moaning once about tourists with cameras, "There is only one thing worse than people asking for pictures, and that is no one asking for pictures." I think Oscar Wilde would have agreed. So, if you see me out and about, don't be shy. Feel free to come up and ask me for a selfie.

If you're having your shoes pissed on, you can either get upset about it, or you can take John Wayne's approach: accept the compliment and stop wearing suede shoes.

I do struggle not to get upset when people who don't know me at all decide who I am and who I'm allowed to be. Ultimately, though, I can't control other people's prejudices and I certainly can't control what journalists choose to write about me. Of course everyone is judged by others all the time, but the downside of being a star is that it is all so much more public, and everybody thinks they're entitled to have a go. It's just part of the territory.

Ever since I played Alfie, parts of the press have found it difficult not to see me as him: a rather uncouth, rather ignorant, chirpy Cockney sparrow, who landed on his feet being cast as uncouth, ignorant, chirpy Cockney sparrows. In the 1960s I was explaining to a journalist that my daughter was called Dominique. "Oh," he said. "You named her after the Singing Nun, did you?" (In 1963 there had been a rather strange number-one hit called "Dominique," performed by a group of singing Belgian nuns.)

"No," I said. "She was named after Dominique Francon, the heroine of the Ayn Rand novel *The Fountainhead*."

He looked stunned. "I've never read that," he said. And why, he seemed to be saying, would this ignorant Cockney bastard have read it?

Britain is much less uptight about class than it used to be but every so often I still get a whiff of it. My current home is a two-hundred-year-old tithe barn that we lovingly and at great expense converted. It is the same traditional style of barn that Tesco then used for its huge supermarkets in the middle of the English countryside. The idea was to make them sympathetic to their environment. One snobbish journalist visiting us told his readers that Michael Caine had built his house to look like a supermarket—the only-just-unsaid assumption being that someone like me would be incapable of having decent taste.

And I was interviewed by an English journalist not long ago who said that I had been wonderful as a butler in *Batman Returns*. "Thank you very much," I said.

And then he added, "But, of course, servants are easier to play, aren't they?" These are small and silly comments and I try not to take them seriously.

And, of course, there are the critics: the professional critics who have a job of work to do, and the people who are just out to put you down. That is all part of living a very public life. Everyone is going to have an opinion about you, and some of those opinions will be expressed quite woundingly.

The important thing here is to try to stay tuned in to people whose opinions matter, and to try to ignore those whose opinions do not—whether they're singing your praises or kicking you in the balls. I desperately needed good publicity early on in my career and scoured the reviews for every word about me. I remember when *The Ipcress File* came out in 1965: I went out and bought all the newspapers and brought them back to my little London flat. The first review I read was terrible and plunged me into the depths of despair. But the next was good, the one after that even better, and finally as I read rave after rave I started to cry uncontrollably—great heaving sobs and finally howls of pent-up ambition and relief. Those reviews really mattered. Later I learnt to steer well clear of my reviews because they were often quite hurtful. The only critics I took any notice of were Dilys Powell in *The Sunday Times*, Pauline Kael in the *New Yorker* and Mark Kermode in the *Guardian* and on Radio 5. If they said a movie was a dud then it probably was. Now there is just no point in reading them. A great review won't help me, and a bad one won't destroy me.

Nevertheless, my ability to ignore the both the bouquets and brickbats was sorely tested very recently.

In 2016, *GQ* magazine, as part of its annual Men of the Year Awards, made me its Legend of the Year. I was stunned and utterly delighted. A week later, Shakira and I were walking down Bond Street and someone approached us. "I read that *GQ* magazine has called you a legend," he said. "It's not true. You're a god." And off he went. Shakira and I stood there flabbergasted for a moment, then both burst out laughing. Meanwhile, at almost exactly the same time, a popular newspaper decided—I don't know why—to publish a long piece on the fifteen worst films I had ever made. (No need to look it up, I'll tell you what the article decided they were: *The Swarm, The Hand, Water, Beyond the Poseidon Adventure, Ashanti, Blue Ice, On Deadly Ground, Blame It on Rio, Jaws: The Revenge, The Island, The Last Witch Hunter, Bullseye, Mr. Destiny, Journey 2: The Mysterious Island, Austin Powers in Goldmember* and *Quicksand*.) Pages and pages of a "light-hearted guide to Caine's worst howlers." Banter, I think they call it. And mostly I agreed with their choices. It's just that it felt like when someone else criticises your mum. You might agree with them. It might be right on the nail and quite funny. But that doesn't make it OK. In the end, though, I did manage to laugh at it too.

While we're on the subject, another thing that does still get to me a little is the critics' obsession with my accent. If I'm playing a Cockney, the complaint is that I'm always playing the same part, always playing myself: as though all Cockneys are essentially the same. As though Alfred Hitchcock, David Bowie and I are the same person. As if Alfie (a self-centred womaniser), Harry Palmer (a cool-headed MI5 spy) and Jack Carter (a hardened, murderous gangster) are all interchangeable. If I'm not playing a Cockney, the complaint is that my put-on accent isn't authentic enough. This thread has run right through my career, from *Zulu* to *The Cider House Rules*.

On *Zulu,* critics who didn't know me (and therefore didn't know I was a working-class lad) enjoyed my performance and didn't comment on my accent. Only the critics who already knew what I sounded like in real life claimed to be able to hear the private under the officer.

When I first gave my dialogue coach for *The Cider House Rules* my American accent he laughed. "That's wonderful, Michael," he said, "but that's a California accent." That made sense: I'd lived in LA for many years. "You're playing a man from New

England. It's actually much closer to an English accent than it is to a Californian one." I spent hours working on that accent, listening to tapes and wandering around Northampton, Massachusetts, where we were filming, listening to people speak. I might have been complimented on my New England accent by the *New Englander* but in England it got panned for being "too English." What can I say?

I don't mind criticism at all but, like most people, when I get it I want it to be fair and helpful.

I started this chapter with a mention of the glittery world of awards ceremonies. They are part and parcel of stardom and I would struggle to say whether they're a pro or a con. Sometimes they bring a well-deserving individual or team to greater prominence. At others they feel like a popularity contest. It's a mixed bag. Awards ceremonies simply are. In my world, the most sought-after accolade is the Academy Award, or Oscar. Like a lot of things in the movie business, the ceremony itself looks very glamorous but in fact involves a lot of hanging about and tension, wearing uncomfortable clothes and feeling hungry.

Winner or loser, if you're nominated the spotlight will be on you and you will have to try to behave appropriately—to be a generous and humble winner, or a gracious loser. There are baubles to be won in many walks of life and I think the trick is to not take them too seriously either way. Enjoy the moment with good grace if you win, but persuade yourself they're not important if you don't. It's not an easy trick to pull off, especially if you have to find that "loser's smile" in the full glare of the world's press.

I was given my first Best Actor nomination for *Alfie* in 1967, when my friend Paul Scofield won for his brilliant performance as Sir Thomas More in *A Man for All Seasons*. I didn't dream I would win—to the extent that I didn't even go to the ceremony—so I was not too disappointed. At that point I was genuinely honoured simply to be nominated. I did attend the ceremony six years later, in 1973, when I got my second nomination, for *Sleuth*. That year, Marlon Brando won for *The Godfather* and, as an act of protest, sent a young Native American woman called Sacheen Littlefeather to collect the award on his behalf. That time, I was too busy being scared witless to be very upset: for some reason, I had agreed to host part of the ceremony, alongside Rock Hudson, Carol Burnett and Charlton Heston. The whole thing was broadcast live, with comedy writers standing in the wings and writing jokes on the fly. It was the most nerve-racking job I have ever done.

Ten years later in 1983 I was nominated for a third time, for *Educating Rita*. This time the odds were stacked against me as four of the five nominees were British, though I suspect the winner, American actor Robert Duvall, would have won in any case for his role as a burnt-out country singer in *Tender Mercies*. As I headed to the after-show party I braced myself for nodding and smiling my way through a series of commiserations and was then moved to tears when I was greeted instead by a standing ovation. Being honoured by my friends like that meant as much as winning the award itself. I was so touched when Cary Grant came up to me and gave me a hug. "You're a winner here, Michael," he whispered.

It was 1987 when I finally won my first Academy Award, in the Best Supporting Actor category for my role in *Hannah and Her Sisters*, and I wasn't even there. The film had been released in February and I had been so sure I would not be nominated (Woody Allen was famously anti-Oscar) that I had not even put the ceremony date in my diary. So, in a terrible piece of luck, I was unavoidably absent, on a ten-day shoot for *Jaws: The Revenge*. The only nomination that won me was one for Worst Supporting Actor at the Golden Raspberry Awards the following year.

By 2000 when I was nominated for Best Supporting Actor for *The Cider House Rules* I had learnt my lesson and I was actually there. As everyone knows, time is of the essence in acceptance speeches, and if you go on too long, the music cuts you off. I had been nominated alongside Tom Cruise, Jude Law, Michael Clarke Duncan and Haley Joel Osment and wanted to pick them out for a remark. I became aware I was going on a bit long, but I also knew this might be my only chance at an Oscars' acceptance speech and I needed another minute. I glanced to the wings and got a thumbs-up from my friend Dick Zanuck, who was producing that year. Gold dust.

It's nice to be nice. It also pays off sometimes. In my acceptance speech, when I mentioned Tom Cruise, who had been nominated for his part in *Magnolia*, I told him he should be pleased he didn't win, as the dressing-room trailers given to supporting actors would be too small and modest for him. It was a joke. But the next movie I shot was *Miss Congeniality*, produced by and starring Sandra Bullock, who was an absolute joy to work with and a true star. She was playing an FBI agent going undercover as a beauty queen. I was the beauty pageant coach—a kind of Professor Higgins role. When I was shown to my trailer on the first day, it was the biggest and most luxurious trailer I had ever seen. On the door was pinned a handwritten note from Sandra: "Welcome to the shoot. This is as big as Tom's." And it was.

Sandra Bullock, by the way, is one of the most pleasant, hard-working and talented people working in the movies today, and a master at the art of gracious winning and losing. I remember in 2010 she won the Best Actress Oscar for her role in *The Blind Side*. The night before that she had won the Golden Raspberry Award for Worst Actress in a film called *All About Steve*. She turned up to both events, and conducted herself with the same grace and humour at both.

My most recent nomination was for *The Quiet American* in 2003. At the time I felt this had been a performance of a lifetime for me. It is still one of the roles of which I'm most proud: where I got closest to making myself disappear and truly becoming someone else. But the timing was way off. So soon after 9/11, and just four days after the U.S. invaded Iraq, a movie even slightly critical of U.S. foreign policy did not stand a chance.

Much as I would love to say that I no longer care about awards, I actually do, a little bit. In 2015 I played a classical-music conductor in a movie called *Youth*, written and directed by the brilliant and tender Paolo Sorrentino. I was very proud of my performance, which I rated as one of the best of my career, and of the movie. *Youth* won Best Film from the European Academy, Paolo Sorrentino won Best Director and I won Best Actor. But the British and American Academies and the Golden Globes ignored the movie, Paolo and me altogether. I was disappointed, I have to admit.

Winner or loser, my favourite bit was always the after-show party where, however famous I might get, I could still get star-struck by my fellow guests. One year I went to the Gents and found myself washing my hands alongside Rupert Murdoch and George Lucas. I'm not sure either of them recognised the other but for me, looking up at the unlikely trio in the mirror in front of me, it was quite surreal.

In my experience, the most surprising thing about becoming a star is that it changes everything and nothing. My life was turned upside down and in many ways transformed, but when I woke up every morning I was still me. The little voice inside my head was still exactly the same. And it was saying: What now? What next?

I like to say, when you reach the top, that's when the climb begins. By all means take some deep breaths and try to capture the view in your mind's eye. Find the perfect spot to sit and eat your sandwiches. But then what? However perfect the spot may be, just sitting there for ever isn't an option. So you either head back down, or consult the map and strike out along the ridge line for that other peak just barely visible in the distance. Even when you think you've finally made it, you aren't going to stop, are you? You're going to carry on. So you'd better make sure you enjoy the journey.

Standing at each of my own personal peaks, I realised that I had to keep climbing. First, because of the obligations I now had to other people. Money for a film would often be raised in my name, and in the expectation of my continuing and reliable presence. On-set, I was expected to carry every scene I was in, oozing star quality. Off-screen, I was needed for interviews, public appearances, promotions, to ensure the picture got as much attention as possible. I have always considered doing publicity for a movie to be part of the deal but, I have to admit, it is one aspect of the business that I have never learnt to love. I suppose I had imagined that being a star would be a bit like being a beautiful tiger, padding sleek and serene through the movie jungle as lesser beasts scrambled to clear my path. It was more like being an old elephant, wearily carrying everything on his back.

And, just as important, I had to keep climbing for myself. Even when I had two movies on release in the United States (*Alfie* and *The Ipcress File*) and an Oscar nomination, even when I had made my first Hollywood movie (*Gambit*), even when I had made dozens of acclaimed movies, even when I had won an Oscar (for *Hannah and Her Sisters*), and then another (for *The Cider House Rules*), I was convinced that I was not going to keep my place up in that firmament unless I kept doing the things that had got me there in the first place. For me, it wasn't so much that I wanted to remain a star. It was that I wanted to keep doing the work I loved. It wasn't the view from the summit but the pleasure in every step. So I kept learning, kept reinventing myself, kept seeking out new challenges, kept on climbing.

12.

Rise and Fall

"Why do we fall, sir? So we can learn to pick ourselves up."

Batman Begins, 2005

OF COURSE, AS I kept climbing, I kept falling. If you think that becoming a star, in the movies or any other universe, means you're never going to fail again—never make poor choices, never fall out of favour, never be involved with something that looks brilliant on paper, then disappoints for no reason anyone can quite put their finger on—then you could not be more wrong.

Those chairs on set with your name on the back are designed to fold up and the names to peel off the backs quite easily. Success is a fleeting moment. It's quicksilver in your hands: beautiful, wonderful, unpredictable and impossible to keep hold of. It's a helium balloon that briefly takes everyone's attention but will always either end up popping spectacularly, or sagging slowly in a corner. It's a child's rainbow soap bubble that gets bigger and bigger, then simply disappears. The path from stardom to disappointment and failure is a well-worn one. I know it well. Even after I'd hit the big-time, my career went through endless ups and downs. When I was up, I was a star with all that went with it. When I was down, a lot of that disappeared.

As the wise Alfred Pennyworth from the *Batman* movies understood so well, to endure and survive, in any walk of life, it is not enough to succeed— to climb to the top. You also need to know, and to learn, how to pick yourself up after you fall. On the many occasions that I fell mid-career, I returned to the lessons I had learnt in the early, brutal years of my career: I learnt from what I could get; I used the difficulty; I looked for blessings in disguise. When I was going through hell, I kept going. I said yes a lot and I gave 100 per cent commitment to every-thing I did. I also learnt some new lessons. It never became any easier but I would go so far as to say I became something of an expert in failure. A success at failing.

👓 *You define your own failures*

To quite a large extent, it is up to you to decide what your own personal success looks like, and your own personal failure. There are people who believe they're making it every day, no matter the reviews or the box office; and there are people who never feel they're making it, no matter how high they rise, or how many little golden men they take home. There are people who are able to say, "That was a disaster," without saying, "I am therefore a failure." And there are people who cannot.

I was eating dinner one evening in Langan's Brasserie, the London restaurant I had opened with Peter Langan in the 1970s, when I was shown a perfect example of how the "never satisfied" people think. There I was at a corner table and a man came by me on the way to the Gents. He was probably a bit pissed. He clocked me, and came over. "I thought you said this place was supposed to be full of film stars?"

I said, "Well, what am I?"

"You own the bloody place," he said. "You're bound to be here."

It was a fair point. I nodded towards the table opposite and said, "Who's that sitting there?"

"Dunno."

"That's Tom Cruise." Then I nodded towards the stairs. "And who's that going up the stairs?"

"Dunno."

"That's Clint Eastwood."

On the way back from the Gents he stopped at my table again. "Well, there was no one famous in the bogs."

That customer had managed to take success and somehow redefine it as failure. I, on the other hand, having learnt from an early age to find the good in even the direst of situations, was generally able to redefine a failure and turn it into some sort of success. A critical flop like *Blame It on Rio* wasn't a failure: it made a lot of money at the box office. *Shiner* wasn't a failure either. It was too brutal for audiences and did not do well at the box office but it got good reviews for the acting. *Bullseye* was disastrous both critically *and* commercially, but it wasn't a failure. I had a great time making it with Michael Winner and Roger Moore. Recently I made a movie that was released straight to DVD, but it was shot in Savannah, Georgia, where our great friend Danny Zarem had been brought up. Shakira and I had been wanting to visit for years.

I even found a way to reconcile myself to *Jaws: The Revenge*. I have never actually watched the movie but I have it on good authority that it was really terrible. I had quite a small part in it, and only worked on it for two weeks, but I was the best-known actor in it so I took a lot of the heat when it was panned by the critics. Not only that but, as you know, my shooting schedule clashed with the Oscars ceremony so I missed picking up my Academy Award for *Hannah and Her Sisters*. What a disaster! What a failure! Except it wasn't, for me. With the money I made on that terrible movie, I bought a more luxurious house for my mother. As I used to say to journalists when they wanted to mock me for this debacle, "I've never seen the movie, but I have seen the house it paid for, and it's fabulous."

I would say that every movie I ever made, whatever its box office, whatever the critics thought, whatever the impact on my professional reputation, in some way enriched my life.

👓 *Reinvent yourself*

If all else fails, change direction. Reinvent "success." Reinvent yourself.

At a point in my career when the movie scripts stopped coming, I went back to TV. Unlike today, with the power of Netflix and Amazon, that was seen as a sign of failure. For me, though, the failure would have been not working at all. I made *Jack the Ripper* in 1988, for which I won a Golden Globe, and *Jekyll and Hyde* in 1990, for which I won both Golden Globe and Emmy nominations. Not a bad way to fail.

At another point, the scripts not only dried up, they started looking hurtfully different. One of the lowest moments of my career—or so it seemed at the time—was that day I was sent the script in which, the producers had to spell out to me, I was to read the father, not the lover. My first reaction to the revelation that I was too old to play the ro-

mantic lead (I was about sixty) was that my acting
career was over and I was going to have to radically
reinvent "success." I moved to Miami, sent back the
few scripts I received, opened a restaurant and settled down to write my autobiography. I told myself
and others that I had retired and that I was happy.
I *was* happy. It wasn't difficult to find good things
about this situation: it was 80 degrees Fahrenheit
in the winter in Miami, my restaurant, South Beach
Brasserie, was thriving, my publishers assured me
my book would sell and I no longer had to get to six
thirty a.m. makeup calls. I'm usually a hard worker
and here was an incredible chance to be lazy.

But I was even happier when Jack Nicholson, a
wonderful actor, who was also in Miami at the time,
persuaded me that the reinvention did not have to
be so extreme. Why not simply reinvent myself as
a movie actor, as opposed to a movie star? A character actor, rather than a leading actor? (What's the
difference? Well, essentially it's this. When movie
stars get a script they want to do, they change it to
suit them. When leading movie actors get a script
they want to do, they change themselves to suit the
script.) Jack brought me a script for a movie called
Blood and Wine and talked me into coming out of
my so-called retirement and going back to work. I
did, and the truth was revealed to me—or I allowed
myself to see it: however happy I kidded myself I

was, I was never going to be happier than when I was acting. Especially with such a great, fun-loving co-star as Jack. Jack is a tremendous actor who, even more than I do, relishes the relaxation. His attitude to work was summed up for me one day when we were hurrying to get a shot before the sun went down. I broke into a light jog to get back to the set. "Don't run, Michael," Jack said to my back laconically. "They'll know it's us who's late." I fell back in line and on we strolled.

That was in 1996. I followed up with *Midnight in Saint Petersburg*, another Harry Palmer movie, another flop for me. But then in 1998 I played the sleazy agent Ray Say in *Little Voice*, a semi-musical starring the brilliant actress and singing impressionist Jane Horrocks, alongside Brenda Blethyn, Ewan McGregor and Jim Broadbent, which was a great success in the UK, if not in the States. And in 1999 I played Dr. Wilbur Larch in *The Cider House Rules*, which starred Charlize Theron, Tobey Maguire and Paul Rudd, and for which I won my second Academy Award. I was off and running again. I was using the difficulty, using my change in status to play a wider range of more interesting, more challenging parts than I had done in my movie-star days. I retired more than twenty years ago, and since then I have made more than forty new movies with a whole new generation of directors, producers and movie stars. I may no longer get the girl, but I'm still getting the parts. Bliss.

👓 *Succeeding enough is enough*

Even since my "retirement" I've made plenty of flops, often with stunning casts and terrific directors. You just never know how these things will go. But I didn't sit around waiting for the great director to give me the perfect script. I kept working. I didn't want it to take five years for my next picture to come along, and then when I got there on Monday morning and someone said "Action," I hadn't acted for five years.

Over and over I repeated the pattern. I made a couple of disappointments but I kept the faith with myself and was always ultimately rewarded, just in time to save myself. *The Magus*, which came out in 1968, was a dire film but I followed it up with *The Italian Job*. Saved. A decade later, *The Swarm, Ashanti* and *Beyond the Poseidon Adventure* were all awful—great on paper, with terrific casts, but awful in reality, yet sprinkled, like magic stardust, in between were *California Suite* with Maggie Smith, who won an Oscar for that performance, and *Dressed to Kill*, in which I played a transvestite killer psychiatrist. Thank you, Brian De Palma, for saving my knicker-covered butt. In the early 1980s *The Island* and *The Hand* were both mediocrities but I followed them up with three successes: *Escape to Victory, Deathtrap* and *Educating Rita.* In the mid-1980s, I snatched victory from the jaws of defeat when *Blame It on Rio* and *The Holcroft Convention* were followed by *Hannah and Her Sisters*, and *Jaws: The Revenge* by *Dirty Rotten Scoundrels.* In the 1990s, after *On Deadly Ground* and *Bullet to Beijing* nearly proved to be the deadly final bullet for my career, Jack Nicholson turned up with *Blood and Wine.*

And, most miraculous of all, in the 2000s, when I'd made a series of unremarkable movies—*The Actors, Secondhand Lions, The Statement*, some so forgettable that I can't remember them myself—a young man turned up on my doorstep one sleepy Sunday morning, unannounced, and script in hand. "Hello, Michael," he said, waving a script in my face. "Sorry to disturb you on a Sunday but I'd like you to read this."

"Oh, hello," I said. "What's your name?"

"Christopher Nolan."

We had never met, but I knew the name. I had seen *Memento*, a fascinating film that Chris had made a few years previously, and loved it. It was the only movie I had ever seen that started at the end and finished at the beginning. "Come in, Christopher," I said, excited that this wonderful young director had brought me a script for what I assumed would be a similar picture: something low-budget and big-potential. I took off my gardening gloves, Shakira made coffee and we sat there, stunned, as Chris explained the script and why he wanted me in the movie. This was not going to be a small arty intellectual piece. Chris was making a series of huge Hollywood blockbusters: a trilogy of Batman movies. "Who do you want me to play in it?" I asked. In my head I had already imagined and then quickly written off Batman, but I thought perhaps I could be a great villain.

"The butler," said Chris.

I hid my disappointment and smiled. "The butler? What do I say? 'Dinner is served'?"

Chris smiled back. "He's not that kind of butler," he said. "Batman is an orphan and the butler is a father to him. It's a very important role."

"OK. Well, leave me the script and I'll read it and send it back to you tomorrow."

"No," said Chris, in what I would come to recognise as his hallmark quiet-but-authoritative manner. "I want you to read it now. I'll wait until you're done and you can tell me yes or no."

"Oh, OK," I said. Obediently I went to my office and read it. And loved it: Alfred Pennyworth, the butler, was a beautifully written role and the whole thing was just fabulous. When I came back, Chris and Shakira were sitting and chatting over more coffee. I said yes, it was handshakes all round and Chris left, taking the script with him.

Thank goodness I'd kept going. Thank goodness I'd trained myself to say yes. There I was, at the age of seventy-one, cast in one of the greatest movie trilogies ever made and about to kick off ten years of movie-making heaven.

🕶 Have a survival kit

Success or failure, we all need our own personal survival kit to see us through. For me, it's feeding the ducks with my three grandchildren. Making chill-out music compilations (I own hundreds of chill-out CDs and I've even made one of my own, *Cained*). The London restaurant scene. Gardening. Cooking. Shakira. My family. Christmas. Making movies is an intense business and I always give it my complete commitment but I never have, and never will, let it become the only source of my happiness or the only way I define my success.

Although I lived in LA for so many years I never held much truck with psychoanalysis. I didn't want to pay good money for someone to tell me what I already knew: I was an actor, so I must by definition be mad. I never consulted astrologers or psychics or fortune-tellers or did any of that. Instead, my best therapy has always been working with my hands, on my own, in peace, designing and growing things in the garden. Maybe it takes me back to the Norfolk farm I was evacuated to during the war.

I have always taken great pleasure in food and in the flowering of the London restaurant scene in the late 1950s, 1960s and every decade since. Until the 1950s, food in England was dull and monotonous, especially for the working class. For us, there was fish and chips, eel and pie and Lyons Corner Houses. There were some good restaurants but they kept the likes of me out with their prices, their stiff suit-and-tie dress codes. I didn't own a suit and tie, and when I asked my dad to buy me one he told me to get a paper round (which I did. And I got a suit. But I still couldn't afford to eat at a posh restaurant). And all the pubs, cafés and public transport closed at ten thirty to ensure the working classes would get up to go to work in the mornings.

I remember trying my first "American hamburger" in Charles Forte's milk bar next to the Empire, Leicester Square. What a joy. Then came the coffee bars, including the 2i's on Old Compton Street, serving coffee and sandwiches and, in the basement for an extra half a crown, rock 'n' roll. I saw Cliff Richard and Tommy Steele for the first time down there. Then came Italian, French, Indian and Chinese restaurants. Eventually in 1976 I opened my own, Langan's Brasserie, based on the brasseries, like La Coupole, that I had seen in Paris as a penniless young man. I had been talking for years about wanting to do it because, despite the flowering of the restaurant scene, there was still nothing like La Coupole in London. There was no dress code, and only one rule for staff behaviour: if I ever saw a waiter looking at their watch in front of a customer, they would be fired immediately.

Later—against the advice of a friend who told me never to trust anyone with names from three different countries—I went into business with a talented young chef called Marco Pierre White, who won three Michelin stars at our restaurant in Knightsbridge, the Marco Pierre White (what else?). I thought movie stars were temperamental but they had nothing on chefs, and one of the invisible costs of doing business with talent like Marco was the installation of extra doors between the kitchen and the restaurant to prevent the customers being exposed to the language that was going into their delicious food. Today London, which was a food desert in the 1950s, has become a gourmet's paradise, with Michelin-starred chefs popping up all over the place and good affordable food from across the world being served up every day. I am proud of my city's culinary revolution and of having been a small part of the change.

I know that golf features in a lot of people's survival kit but there are a couple of reasons it was never going to work for me. The first is Sidney Poitier, who is the kindest, gentlest person you are ever likely to meet. He tried to teach me golf once and I was so bad that he *nearly* lost his temper. The second is Sean Connery. Sean is not the kindest, gentlest person in the world. In fact, he can be very competitive and impatient. And when he tried to teach me golf he became so incensed that he grabbed my club and broke it in two. For the sake of my friendships with these two—oh, yes, I should add friendship to the list of what's in my survival kit—the golf had to go.

But that's fine. It doesn't have to be golf, or gardening, or chill-out. It's whatever can transport you to another place or give you an outlet for a few hours when the going gets tough. When I couldn't redefine failure away, or reinvent my way out of failure, or when I simply had a bad day at the office, my family and friends, and my enthusiasms beyond my career, helped me to keep things in perspective.

👓 *What doesn't help*

I also worked out, through experience, and with a little help from a rather odd group of friends, strangers and loved ones, what was not going to help me survive the difficult times.

There was a point in my career when I used alcohol to manage stress, and perhaps also—despite all the glitz and the glamour—to manage a feeling that something was missing from my life. I used to tell myself that I needed it: the stress would get me before the alcohol would. I was never bombed on set, but I thought that a small vodka for breakfast was nothing to worry about, and by the early 1970s I was drinking two bottles of the stuff a day. By an immense stroke of good fortune, Shakira arrived in my life just in time. The empty feeling vanished and she got on my case. Then, to top it all, she got pregnant and I was given a second go at fatherhood, and soon I'd got myself straightened out. I gave up alcohol entirely for a year and now I never drink during the day, and with dinner it's just wine. Shakira, literally, saved my life.

I know what I could have become if it hadn't been for Shakira because in my time in the theatre, the movies and the restaurant business I have come across my fair share of towering alcoholics, and seen my fair share of careers ruined and lives shortened by alcohol. I saw Richard Burton's *Hamlet* in 1964 and many years later when I met him on the set of *Zee and Company*, where I was working with his then-wife Elizabeth Taylor, I told him it had been wonderful, but the fastest *Hamlet* I had ever seen. He looked at me and said, "The pubs shut at ten thirty." Richard was always very pleasant to me when he was sober, which was almost never. At the end-of-picture party for *Zee and Company* I said happy Christmas to him and Elizabeth as I left. "Why don't you go fuck yourself," he growled back.

A few years later Richard and his new wife Suzy, Sean Connery and his wife Micheline, and Shakira and I were having dinner together in Hollywood somewhere. Suzy told us that Richard had been on the wagon for some time, and I believed it. For the first two courses Richard never said a word, rude or otherwise. Then he went to the toilet and came back obviously very refreshed and started talking at high speed, very enthusiastically, about everybody. I never saw Richard again. Despite all that he achieved he did not fulfil his enormous professional promise and he died in 1984 before he reached the age of sixty.

Peter Langan was a brilliant chef and restaurateur. He made the best spinach soufflé, seafood salad and crème brûlée I've ever tasted, and he taught me that a restaurant should be a piece of theatre. It was not somewhere to come before the show or after the show, it was the show. The walls were the set and needed to be beautifully dressed with expensive-looking artwork—in our case by Peter's friends David Hockney and Patrick Procktor. The tables should be well spaced but the bar should be at the front and crowded, balancing comfort with a sense of excitement and desirability. The customers were both the audience and the stars of the show: everyone had to be able to see everyone else at all times. But Peter was an alcoholic of quite magnificent proportions—he would occasionally get so drunk he insulted the customers. Once he got under a table and bit a woman's leg, and he often ended up sleeping either in the restaurant at a table or rough on the streets. After a few months of working with him I realised I needed a chef who was not only brilliant but also sober, which was how Richard Shepherd became the chef and third partner at Langan's. Peter's restaurant was a great success but ten years after he opened it, at the tragically young age of forty-seven, he was dead.

Perhaps the supreme example was an actor called Wilfred Lawson who played Alfred Doolittle in the film version of *Pygmalion* with Leslie Howard and Wendy Hiller. You may never have heard of him but every British actor of my generation had. He was a true actor's actor, and should have enjoyed a long, sparkling career. I saw Wilfred once in a Shakespeare matinee—I think it was *Richard III* at the Savoy Theatre—with another prodigious drunk, Trevor Howard. They were clearly inebriated and someone in the audience yelled, "You're drunk." Trevor just shouted back, "If you think we're drunk, wait until you see the Duke of Norfolk." I'd love to know who could possibly have been out-drinking those two but sadly I just cannot remember. I worked with Wilfred Lawson on *The Wrong Box* in 1966, a Victorian comedy directed by my great friend Bryan Forbes and with a wonderful best-of-British cast including, among so many others, John Mills, Peter Cook and Dudley Moore. Whenever I did a scene with Wilfred, who was in his sixties by then, Bryan shot from above the waist so that I could hold his hand and guide him steadily to his marks on the floor. Shortly after that I remember coming across Wilfred in the Arts Club in London. He was sitting at the bar learning his lines for a West End play. I asked him when he opened. "Eight o'clock tonight," he said.

I always maintain that it was drugs that brought the 1960s to an end. All that creative energy turned into a lot of sitting around, spaced out. I only did drugs of any kind once, or they could have been the end of me too. A friend gave me some marijuana and I laughed for about five hours and nearly gave myself a hernia. I was trying to get a cab home from Grosvenor Square to Notting Hill at about one in the morning and was standing on the corner laughing like a lunatic. Nothing would stop for me and

I ended up walking all the way home. When I got back I vowed that was my first and last time, and it was. It wasn't just the hernia or the walking for miles. I knew that marijuana affected memory and I had lines to learn.

Of course everything is much more efficient now. These days, shiningly talented young men and women who would once have taken decades to slowly poison themselves with alcohol can get themselves addicted to drugs that will kill them in a matter of months. I well remember Hollywood parties where I had to be stopped from putting sugar in my coffee: "Don't do that, Michael. It's cocaine." Or where I nearly peed myself trying to find a bathroom that wasn't otherwise occupied. If I hadn't realised the dangers already, they were brought brutally home to me with the death from an accidental drugs overdose of that effervescent talent Heath Ledger at the age of twenty-eight. Just months earlier we had been shooting together on the second of Chris Nolan's *Batman* movies, *The Dark Knight*. I had been concerned that no one would be able to follow Jack Nicholson's performance as the Joker in Tim Burton's *Batman* movie, but Heath, charming, gentle and thoughtful off-camera, had blown us all away with his utterly original, deeply disturbing, yet nuanced and witty interpretation of the role, for which he received a well-deserved posthumous Oscar. What a loss. What a waste.

Alcohol could have killed my career as it killed so many others. Eighty cigarettes a day, which was what I was smoking in the 1960s, weren't going to kill my career—or not directly. But try having a career when you're dead. I gave up drinking in a matter of months, thanks to Shakira. It took almost thirty years for me to give up smoking, thanks to a motley and unlikely crew made up of Tony Curtis, Yul Brynner and Hurricane Higgins.

In 1971, not long before I first met Shakira, I was at a posh party in Mayfair, standing by a fire chatting to someone and smoking my usual Gitanes cigarettes, lighting my next fag from the dog end of the last. I felt a hand go inside my jacket pocket, take out my cigarette packet and throw it onto the fire. I swivelled around, about to protest, and there behind me was Tony Curtis. I had never met him before but he was extremely famous, not least for his brilliant turn in *Some Like It Hot*. I said, "What did you do that for?" and Tony said, "You're going to die, Michael, if you keep doing that, you idiot." He proceeded to give me a very clinically detailed and convincing argument about the risks of smoking. Then he walked away, having (one-third) saved my life in about a minute and a half. I never smoked cigarettes again.

I did, though, take up cigars, thinking they were safer. Then one night many years later I was at a dinner party at Gregory Peck's house in Los Angeles and found myself, after the ladies had retired to the living room, sitting next to Yul Brynner, smoking my cigar. (Dinner parties in LA were often rather formal affairs.) I offered one to Yul, who declined. "No thanks," he said quietly. "I have lung cancer. I'll be dead in two months."

I immediately started to smash my cigar out in an ashtray. "I'm sorry, I'm sorry," I said. "I'll put it out."

"Don't bother on my account," said Yul, putting his hand on my arm. "It's too late for me." That night, he looked healthy and powerful but, sure enough, within a few months he was dead. I gave up cigars for a year or so after that, then went back to them, telling myself that Yul had smoked cigarettes and I was smoking cigars—so much less harmful. That was two-thirds of my life saved.

Finally, in 2003, just before my seventieth birthday I was watching TV, cigar in hand (on my own in my office because the rest of the family couldn't stand the smell). On came the snooker player Hurricane Higgins, speaking through a voice-box and looking absolutely terrible, making an anti-smoking commercial. He had throat cancer. I put my cigar down in the ashtray and have not smoked since. Thank you, Tony, thank you, Yul, thank you, Hurricane. And may your souls rest in peace.

Don't be frightened of failure. I have found failure to be a great teacher, whose lesson is "Don't do that again." I took that advice many times, and I failed again many times, but always for a different reason. And failure can happen to anyone. I like to say that I have made flops with some of my best friends and some of the most talented people in the business. Norman Jewison, director of *Fiddler on the Roof, In the Heat of the Night* and *Moonstruck*, directed me in *The Statement*, set in beautiful Aix-en-Provence but not beautiful in any other way. Oliver Stone, genius director of *JFK* and *Platoon*, directed me in *The Hand*, a horror picture in which the star of the show is my severed hand. Nora Ephron, writer of *When Harry Met Sally* and writer-director of *Sleepless in Seattle*, directed me in *Bewitched*, which, somehow, just didn't work. And Irwin Allen, the extremely talented producer of *The Poseidon Adventure* and *The Towering Inferno*, was the first-time director of *The Swarm*. I was in *Ashanti* with Peter Ustinov and Omar Sharif, in *Curtain Call* with Maggie Smith, *The Jigsaw Man* with Laurence Olivier and *Bewitched* with Nicole Kidman. There were no recriminations. In fact, whenever I see Oliver Stone he likes to say to me, "Michael, the best movie you ever made was *The Hand*." I got enormous pleasure from working with every one of them and, spending time with every one of them, I had moments I wouldn't exchange for anything in the world—and we're all still friends.

The only way to be sure you never fail is never to do anything at all. And the only way to really, truly fail is not to learn from your failures. Any time you learn from a failure, it's a success.

13.

Being Decent

"I know I am behaving badly, but I have every intention of behaving badly. As a matter of fact, this is exactly the kind of situation where one should behave badly."

The Quiet American, 2002

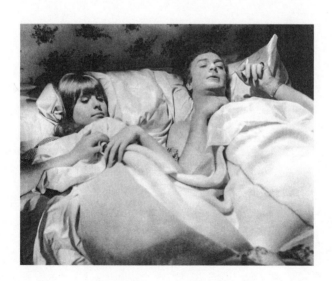

BEING A DECENT HUMAN being is difficult for everyone from time to time but it seems there are particular challenges for those who become stars in their worlds. In some ways, being decent becomes harder, just at the point when your behaviour becomes more noticeable and more important. Harder, because once you enter that bubble of stardom you can lose touch with reality and become demanding, egotistical and unreasonable almost as a way of life. More noticeable, because everyone is watching, all the time. We love to know what famous people are "really" like. Did you lose your rag in an airport queue? Or did you take time out of your day to smile at a little boy, sign an autograph and tell him to be good for his mum? Either way, whoever witnesses it will extrapolate an entire personality for you, and tell all their friends. More important, because the more successful you become, the more your behaviour sets the tone for everyone around you.

👓 *Stay grounded*

Some huge stars completely lose touch with the real world. Frank Sinatra, for example, was an extremely generous member of the secret philanthropists' club of Hollywood—a circle of big stars who took care of less successful actors as they grew older or fell on hard times—and became a great friend of mine. But he was a law unto himself and everything was on his terms. For example, Frank had a Twenty Minute Rule. He would not travel for dinner more than twenty minutes' drive from his house in Beverly Hills. If he had been invited to dinner and had been in the car for twenty minutes he would command his driver to turn around. "I'm twenty minutes," he would call out. "It's too far. We're going home." Mind you, he was also known to fly to Paris for dinner when he was staying in London. And he would always have people fussing around him.

I remember once one of his guys whispered to me conspiratorially, "Frank's in a great mood today."

I said, at normal volume, "What about me? What about my mood?"

And the guy looked at me like I was crazy. "Who cares? No one cares how you feel."

I have known stars who have demanded private planes, drugs, full interior design for their trailers. It goes on.

I was lucky. I always had my family to keep me grounded. There's nothing like your mum saying she's had enough of LA and wants to go home to London to catch up on her favourite soap, or your wife saying, "You want a cup of tea? Sure, the kettle's over there," to remind you that no matter how much adulation and validation you're getting in your professional world, at home you're just plain old you. Not a star, not a god and quite possibly not the person who has had the hardest day.

The other people who have always kept me grounded are taxi drivers. In fact, I sometimes think Shakira keeps a few cab drivers on retainer just to stop me getting too big-headed. The other day, I got into a cab to go out for dinner and the driver, who must have been about fifty, looked in his mirror and said, "My grandfather loved you. He saw all your films." There was a little pause. "He's dead now."

"Oh," I said. "Have you seen any?"

"I don't think so."

On the way back I got into a different cab. I saw the driver clock me in his mirror. "Hey, I know you," he said. I nodded encouragement. I was hoping for something about how brilliant I'd been in *Batman*. Instead: "Didn't you used to be Michael Caine?"

Alec Guinness, that great British theatre and film

actor, perhaps best-known for his role as Obi-Wan Kenobi in the original *Star Wars* movies, but also acclaimed for his work with the greatest director of his era, David Lean, in films like *Great Expectations, Oliver Twist* and *The Bridge on the River Kwai*, told me he had similar luck with cabbies. He once got into the back of a cab and the driver said, "I know you." Alec opened his mouth to confirm that he was indeed Alex Guinness and the driver said, "No, don't tell me. I'll get it. Before you get out, I'll get your name." As Alec was paying the fare, the driver said with a flourish, "I've got it. Telly Savalas."

So Alec says, "No, that's not it."

"I bet you wish you was, though," says the cabbie. Alec nodded, with a rueful Obi-Wan smile, and walked off into the night.

ᗡ *Pay it forward/create an atmosphere*

I still remember, viscerally, how nerve-racking it was being an extra or bit-part actor and I still remember the encounters with my idols that made me feel like a million dollars. Some, like Frank Sinatra, Sidney Poitier and Gregory Peck, eventually became close friends. Others took me under their wing and let me learn from them for the duration of a shoot: Noël Coward, for example, who did a hilarious turn as a gangster boss in *The Italian Job*, was a gloriously unstuffy, unfussy master of comic timing, who very sweetly used to take me for dinner at the Savoy Grill every Wednesday evening when we were shooting. Noël had come from unpromising beginnings south of the river, worked hard, cultivated an image and completely invented himself: he was an inspiration to me and I couldn't believe I had the chance to get to know him a little. He was also warm, witty and a wonderful dinner companion. I remember one evening we got on to the subject of Vanessa Redgrave, who was in the news at the time because she was leading protests against the Vietnam War. "She will keep *on* demonstrating," said Noël. "But, then, she's a very tall girl and I suppose she's pleased to sit down." Then others, like Sophia Loren and William Holden, spoke to me when I had an uncredited bit part in their 1958 movie *The Key*, and Vivien Leigh, one of my all-time favourite actors, simply exchanged a few kind and encouraging words with me.

I only met Vivien once, in 1966, on a memorable London evening when John Gielgud came over and introduced himself to me and told me that he and his dinner companion—a tiny woman in dark glasses—had just seen *Alfie* and loved it. The tiny woman whipped off her glasses and there, in the living, breathing flesh, was Vivien Leigh. I was about to begin shooting *Hurry Sundown*, for which I was going to need a Southern American accent, so I took a deep breath and seized the moment to get an acting lesson from one of my biggest acting idols. "How did you do your accent for *Gone with the Wind?*" I asked.

"Oh," smiled Vivien, "it's easy." She was being really sweet to an annoying young actor and gave no sense that she had been asked this question hundreds of times before. "I just said 'four-door Ford' over and over." Only she pronounced it "foah-doah Fohd." So if you think I sounded like Scarlett O'Hara in that movie, that's the reason why.

I remember, too, some of the thoughtful little acts that made a big difference to a nervous young actor. When I was preparing to act opposite Laurence Olivier in *Sleuth,* there was one small, rather English matter that was bothering me. Formally, Laurence Olivier was Lord Olivier. So what should I call him? Was I going to have to address the only other actor on set as "Lord Olivier" or, even more medieval, "my lord"? Larry had the imagination and grace to anticipate my concern and he wrote to me before shooting began. "You may be wondering how to address me when we meet," he wrote. "From the moment we shake hands I will be Larry forever more." Phew. One less thing to worry about.

Of course, I also still remember the other kinds of

encounters with big movie stars that left me feeling despondent, furious or a bag of nerves.

When I was a bit-part actor, John Mills had me fired from a movie set for being too tall. I turned up to do my first scene with him, and he said he was sorry but he couldn't act while looking up. He did at least insist I got my full fee, and we later became friends and even acted together in *The Wrong Box* a few years later: apparently John was prepared to look up once my star had risen a little higher.

Around the same time, Oliver Reed and I got small two-day parts in a Norman Wisdom film called *The Bulldog Breed*. I was an uncredited sailor and Oliver was an uncredited Teddy Boy. Apart from our dialogue with him, Norman never spoke to either of us and, in fact, he ordered the assistants to keep the pair of us away from him. What a conceited, nasty man: not funny at all.

Elizabeth Taylor was delightful and utterly professional, but she had been a star since childhood and the behaviour of her retinue when we were shooting *Zee and Company* together in 1970 almost gave me a nervous breakdown. Every morning we were given a running commentary on her Royal Progress. "She's just left the hotel...The car's pulling up outside...She's in Makeup...She's in Hair...She's *on her way*!"

I make a point of treating everyone on set or

on location equally—the stars, the unknowns, the crew, the tea boy. On the first day, I introduce myself to everyone as Michael. I don't want people to think I'm swanning about, assuming they all know who I am. And I don't want people worrying: "Bloody hell, what do I call him? Mr. Caine? Sir Michael?" It's "Hello, my name is Michael" to everyone. I don't pull rank. I much prefer to make friends with everyone and create a happy, relaxed atmosphere, to put everyone at their ease. I want everyone to feel "I'm fabulous, we're all fabulous." I want the feeling in the whole unit to be one of excitement at our common endeavour. It's the right thing to do and it's also the best thing to do. I know that how I behave on set will make a difference to everyone's day, and everyone's performance.

If there is a young or inexperienced actor on set who is clearly nervous, I immediately go to work on them, like some kind of nanny. I think back to what I would have wanted to hear, back when I was screwing up my lines and knocking over the furniture, and say and do whatever I can to put them at ease: tell silly jokes, distract them with my acting tips, describe how I always used to mess up my lines, reassure them that it doesn't matter if they do—"We'll just do it again." I have even occasionally made deliberate mistakes so they don't feel like they're the only ones.

Encouraging young actors is not just altruism on my part. It's a two-way street and the honour is often mine. At a dinner for the premiere of *Educating Rita* in Hollywood, back in the 1980s, my wife Shakira left the seat beside me to talk to a friend and I found that a young man I didn't recognise had sat himself down next to me. "Excuse me, Michael," he said, "I wonder if you could give me some advice." I don't remember what I said, but we talked for about ten minutes and then Shakira reappeared. He jumped out of the chair immediately and started to walk away.

"What's your name?" I called after him.

"Tom Cruise," he said, opening his face into his trademark smile. That was the year that a twenty-one-year-old Tom broke out in *The Outsiders* and *Risky Business*, so whatever it was I said to him, I'm sure he needed no advice from me.

Still on the topic of extraordinary young talent, a few years ago I was playing the part of Austin Powers's father, Nigel Powers, in *Austin Powers in Goldmember.* At the first production cast meeting I met our leading lady, a very beautiful, very self-possessed, unknown-to-me African American woman who, I later discovered, was just nineteen years old. I started to talk to her and she told me that she was in a singing group I had never heard of, and that this was her first movie but her ambition was to be an actress and win an Oscar. "Good for you, darling," I said. "What's your name?"

"Beyoncé Knowles," she said. Beyoncé was quiet, observant and completely professional, with a sensitive regard for the feelings of everyone else on set. It was a pleasure and a privilege to work with this young star and, though I know her trophy cabinet is already heaving, I wouldn't rule out that Academy Award just yet.

I have only once had anyone fired and it was early in my career before I knew better. I was being driven to Pinewood Studios the first day of filming on *The Ipcress File*. The chauffeur, who must have been spoiling for a fight, opened up with "Are you the star of this film?" I said I was. "Have you read the book?" I said I had. "Biggest piece of shit I've ever read," he said. I was furious. I indicated that I would prefer to drive the rest of the journey in silence, and as soon as we arrived at the studio, I fired him. I recognise now that that came from a mixture of uncontrolled anger and insecurity. I'm not proud of it, it didn't make me feel better and I've never done it again.

I would never have anyone fired but I am careful about who I choose to work with.

Once when I was visiting New York I went to the hotel suite of a well-known and very successful comedy actor to discuss a movie we were thinking of making together. He was going to be the star, and I was going to be the second star. I hadn't especially liked this guy on screen, but it was a good part for lots of money and his hotel was next door to mine, right by Central Park, so I thought I'd at least meet him. I went into his suite and he said, "Hello, Michael, have a seat." I sat down and we looked at each other. There was a silence, which seemed to go on for a long time although it probably didn't. Finally the actor said, "It's not going to work, is it, Michael?"

I shook my head. "No." I said. "I don't think you like me, and I'm afraid I don't like you either." He nodded. "It was a pleasure meeting you," I lied, and I got up and walked out.

For the most part, successful actors are not temperamental. The industry requires too much discipline: six thirty makeup calls and a lot of standing around while the cameras, the lights and the sound get happy. And sticking your nose in the air and insisting on special treatment is the kind of thing that leads to hammers and lamps falling perilously close to your head.

But I do know one huge star who insists nobody can look her in the eye when she is working, or start a conversation with her. Imagine the eggshells everyone is walking on all day. I can't think they're doing their best work, even if she is.

I've known another who has deliberately kept a whole cast and crew waiting all morning to make a point. I was working on a movie with a male star who was very jealous of his time while he was shooting. One day he was called to the set and kept waiting around. I forget why: the light was wrong, or the weather changed or something. One of those things that happen a lot. The following morning he sent a message to say, "Because you kept me waiting for four hours yesterday, I'm going to be four hours late today." There was nothing we could shoot without him so we, the entire cast and crew, sat twiddling our thumbs for four hours. When he finally turned up, everyone looked at me to see what I would do. I think they were hoping I'd have a big row with him, and it's true, I was absolutely furious. But instead I pointedly took him into a corner, put my hand on his shoulder and said, "I just want to say thank you. I was out all night last night and I hadn't learnt my dialogue. Now I've had a fabulous nap, I've learnt my lines and I'm feeling great. In fact, it just occurs to me: I'm going to a party tonight so can you be late again tomorrow? That way I won't be the one getting into trouble." He wasn't late the next day, or any other day.

I don't like working with temperamental actors and I try to protect my colleagues from them too. If an actor is having a tantrum and throwing their weight around on set, I go home until everything has calmed down. That is a big, expensive drag. It usually means that either they leave the movie or I do. And I have never left a movie. When you become a star, you enter a world where you can pretty much say what you want and usually get it. Stamping and screaming becomes, in fact, much less necessary. Some see it as a signal of their stardom. I see it as a signal of not-quite-stardom and insecurity, often followed by complete anonymity.

Who are the nicest people working in Hollywood today? I'd have to include Sandra Bullock, Woody Harrelson, Scarlett Johansson, Charlize Theron, Jack Nicholson, Steve Martin and Jude Law. They're all actors of huge talent, but beyond that, they're people you want to work with. They work hard, they have a laugh, they learn their lines, they don't upset anybody. Basically, they don't take themselves too seriously.

👓 *Keep your temper*

The irony of all this is that I have a terrible temper myself. But these days I never lose it and I never allow anyone else to lose theirs either.

The last time I blew my top on a movie set was in 1970 when I was making *The Last Valley*, directed by James Clavell and co-starring Omar Sharif. *The Last Valley* was, like many others of that era, a war movie, but with a difference: it was set in the seventeenth century, during the Thirty Years War. I was playing the captain of a mercenary force and, unfortunately for me, that meant horses.

My daughter Dominique was by now an expert horsewoman and, knowing my unhappy history with and sheer terror of horses after my *Zulu* debacle, had given me some advice: I should ask for a docile mount and stipulate that it should be a mare. Imagine my surprise and delight when I was shown to my horse—the biggest I had ever seen and very obviously a stallion. His name was something Germanic that was translated for me to "Fury." "No, no," I was assured, when I raised a query. "He's as quiet as can be and was chosen with you in mind." I had a few practice rides and Fury did indeed seem to be a gentle soul. Until the first day of shooting, that was. I had got into my costume and thought Fury and I would go for a little trot. The trot quickly became a canter, and the canter became a gallop. Hanging on to Fury's mane for dear life, I really thought I was going to die. Eventually we were brought to a screaming halt (it was me doing the screaming) by a jeep from the unit, about two miles from the set.

As soon as I got back to the set I went ape

shit at everybody, yelling and screaming until my voice was hoarse. Jimmy Clavell waited until I had shouted myself out, then dismissed the crew for two hours, sat me down and gave me one of the most useful lessons of my life. "I was a prisoner of the Japanese during the war," he said to me, very quietly and calmly, "and the reason I survived and others did not is that I never lost face. If you lose your temper in front of people you do not know, you are displaying a most intimate emotion in front of strangers. You look a fool and you feel a fool. You lose their respect and it is almost impossible to win it back. You must keep control. If you cannot control yourself, you look weak, and you have no chance of controlling others. And, by the way, the reason your horse ran away was that your sword was slapping against his side. Every time he felt that sword on his side he thought you were urging him to go faster. Now, you are going to have to apologise to everyone on set."

He was right. I did apologise and from that time on I have never lost my temper on a set, no matter what happens. I have also never got back on a horse and nothing and no one could tempt me to do so.

Actually, I did lose it just once recently. Daniel Radcliffe was doing an interview a couple of years ago about *Now You See Me 2*, a very fun heist movie where the robbers are brilliant magicians. When he was asked what it was like working with me, he said I still seemed to love my job despite my advanced age, and that "the only time he got remotely irate was when a camera smacked him in the head." Even then I only got angry with an inanimate object. I would never, ever shout at anyone less powerful than me. It is not just about losing face: it would be hideously unfair.

If you anger me, or cross me, you will never see me lose my temper. James Clavell taught me that. In fact, you will never see anything, because you would just disappear from my life. My parents taught me that. My dad taught me never to let anyone have two goes at me. And my mum taught me that the worst thing you can do to an enemy is to ignore him. To be angry is to be a victim. To move on is the only victory.

👓 Staying the right side of the line

For actors there is one kind of scene above all others where it is most important to behave properly and treat colleagues with respect: the love scene.

This is a fraught area for almost every actor and actress, and rich pickings for anyone intent on behaving badly, but in my experience it is straightforward to behave like a decent human being. My approach was always to stay as professional as possible. I abandoned my usual mantras of "be prepared" and "be real" and I just kept things very respectful and very proper.

I do not recommend getting together and "breaking the ice" before shooting. Rehearse, yes, if you must. But no one thinks that if you have a fight scene in a movie you should go out and beat each other up the night before, and love scenes are no different.

When I was making *Alfie* my co-star Shelley Winters, with whom I had a lot of pretty racy scenes, appeared to take a different approach. I was a relative unknown at that point while Shelley was already a big Hollywood name. The first time I set eyes on her, she was thundering down a corridor of the Dorchester Hotel in London where we were due to shoot a location scene. It was eight o'clock on a Monday morning and I was just heading into Makeup when I caught sight (and sound) of her and thought I'd introduce myself. "Well, hello, Michael," boomed Shelley, grinning widely. "I'm so pleased to meet you. Let's do it before we go into Makeup, shall we? Otherwise we'll have to get made-up all over again."

"Do what?" I asked, in genuine puzzlement.

"Screw, of course," she said, eyes a-twinkle. "I always like to screw the leading man on the first day.

It gets it out of the way. Otherwise all that sexual tension can interfere with the performance. Don't you think?"

I was frozen to the spot and speechless for a moment, then turned on my heels and fled. As I did, I heard her laughter echoing down the corridor. She was just messing.

I don't mess, but I do tend to make jokes at my own expense, to keep the atmosphere light and to avoid the actress getting the impression that I'm enjoying myself too much. As soon as the director says, "Cut!" I'm out of character and making a joke to make it clear to my co-star that the passion is all an act. Elizabeth Taylor and I found an alternative approach: we compared our old scars. I had two and she had six.

One other little thing, born of experience: I carry mouth spray and have a quick squirt just before a kissing scene. The actress will usually say, "What's that?" and I say, "Here you go," and give her a squirt. That way we're both covered.

Most actors and most actresses find love scenes, especially bedroom scenes, embarrassing. Most people I know get nervous. Julie Walters had a novel approach to dealing with the nerves. She once managed to con the entire shooting unit into taking their own clothes off, by telling them it was a new ruling from the actors' union, Equity. On *Blue Ice,*

Sean Young had to do a short nude scene and made the (all-male) crew strip down to their underpants. Don't try this in the office.

There are exceptions, though. Glenda Jackson, who was my co-star in the 1975 British film *The Romantic Englishwoman* and an extraordinary actress, not only always seemed in complete command of the situation, she actually seemed to enjoy it. She walked around the set naked all the time, even when we weren't shooting the nude scenes. Didn't give a toss.

There must have been something in the air on that movie because actually Glenda wasn't the only one. On the first morning on set, another member of the cast, a young actress, came into my dressing room naked and asked me for a cigarette. I was married, and scared. I said nothing. I just gave her the cigarette and lent her a towel for her walk back down the corridor.

I have done love scenes with some of the great beauties and great actresses of my time: Elizabeth Taylor, Jane Fonda, Jane Asher, Shelley Winters, Glenda Jackson, Maggie Smith. I cherished these moments, but I never became confused. I remembered that these women were not beautiful women who happened to be in bed with me—or not only that—but primarily brilliant actors who had a job of work to do, just as I did. And if I can stay professional in these situations, if I can see a clear line between what is and what is not acceptable, if I can behave when my office is also a bedroom, then everyone else can too. It is not that difficult. Those who claim it is are just not trying hard enough.

I have to say, though, that the best love scene I've ever performed was as Alfred Pennyworth saying goodbye to Batman in *The Dark Knight Rises*. And I got to keep all my clothes on.

14.

Don't Look Back (with a Few Exceptions)

Daniel Dravot: "Peachy, I'm heartily ashamed for gettin' you killed instead of going home rich like you deserved to, on account of me bein' so bleedin' high and bloody mighty. Can you forgive me?"

Peachy Carnehan: "That I can and that I do, Danny, free and full and without let or hindrance."

Daniel Dravot: "Everything's all right then."

The Man Who Would Be King, 1975

WRITING A BOOK LIKE this inevitably involves some reflection. But until this point in my life a principle that has served me well is to avoid "looking back on my little life," and keep facing forwards. I don't like to mull over what's behind me: it's a waste of time, because there's nothing I can do about it. I like to plan ahead. I'm always making plans for the future: reading new scripts, planting new trees. As I say to my grandchildren, "Don't look back, you'll trip over."

👓 *Don't watch the rushes*

When I'm shooting a scene, my concentration is absolute. I don't think about the last shot and what I could have done better. I don't think about the next shot and fiddle about with it in my mind. I give myself entirely to what I need to be doing in this moment. And then, when the shot is done, it's done. I don't worry about how I looked or how I did. Once the director is happy, I wipe it from my mind and move on.

It's a great approach except when it comes to what's known as post-synching. This is where, sometimes months after a shoot, an actor is called back in to redo the voice for a particular scene. Maybe a dog barked or maybe the director has decided he wants a different inflection. I've usually done another film or two by this point and it takes a lot of work to remember my character, my accent, what I'm supposed to be feeling in that particular scene. I much prefer to get it right the first time. Leaving it for later can seem tempting when things aren't going well on the day, but almost invariably it is a mistake: in the end it is harder work for a slightly diminished performance.

So, I focus completely on the shot we're taking now and try to get it right first time. For similar reasons, I never watch the rushes. Why ruin today worrying about yesterday? Much better to spend that time getting it right today and preparing for tomorrow.

Rushes are the bits of film from one day's shooting that are processed and "rushed" back for the director and others to look at, to check things are going as they should. Although, these days, there is no processing or rushing. Everyone can just head round to a little van behind the camera and view the footage as soon as it has been shot.

I learnt my lesson about not watching rushes very early on. When I was making *Zulu*, my first big movie, we were shooting on location in South Africa and the film had to be sent back to England to be processed. So, we had been shooting for two weeks by the time the first rushes came back. (The rushes took so long they really should have been called meanders.) The stakes were high as the entire cast and crew crammed themselves into a screening room and the projectors whirred into action. My heart was pounding and my palms were slick with sweat. The screen flickered and was filled with a huge pink face, which I realised to my horror was me, while someone (also me) started droning on in a ridiculously clipped British accent. Behind me I heard a titter and then, "Who told that silly bastard to pull his hat down over his fucking eyes?" The hat thing had been a carefully planned piece of characterisation. I had decided to wear my old-fashioned peaked military pith helmet low, shading the top half of my face, for most of the time, and to tip my head back to allow the sun to catch my eyes when I wanted to make a particular point. Bitterly disappointed that my career was going to be over so soon, I ran out of the room and threw up.

I wasn't involved in shooting the next day, so I

spent it tying myself in stomach-clenching knots. That evening I decided I had to face the music and go down to the hotel bar to let Cy Endfield and Stanley Baker tell me I had been fired. By the time they arrived back from the day's shooting I was a couple of drinks in, with a couple more lined up on the bar. "Hey, not bad, kid," said Stanley, as they breezed by. "Don't worry—you'll get better." I just stood there and looked after them with my mouth open.

So, no more rushes for me. I don't want to screw up today's work and tomorrow's worrying about yesterday's. And I don't want to focus on what it looks like on the outside when the performance has to come from within me. I want to be in the moment, now, getting it right from the inside. And it's not just that. When the rushes go well, that can be an unhelpful distraction too. You have to remember that just as all I saw in the *Zulu* rushes was my own big sweating head, everyone else was seeing only *their* work. If you ask Makeup how the rushes were, they'll say, "Wonderful. Her eye liner looked amazing." If you ask Costume, they'll say, "Amazing. The colour on that shirt really pops."

And actors can get so fixated on the rushes that they start performing for each other. *Harry and Walter Go to New York* was a 1976 comedy starring James Caan and Elliott Gould, with Diane Keaton and me supporting. Diane was like me, she didn't go to the rushes, but we would sometimes sit together in tense silence outside the screening room, straining to hear whether there were any laughs. All through the shoot, everyone was so pleased, because everyone in the screening room never stopped pissing themselves. They would come out almost sick they had laughed so hard. But when real people saw it, there wasn't a single laugh. James and Elliott had been cracking each other up and having a great time, but no one else seemed to get the joke.

Everyone can convince themselves that because they have done their best work or their co-star cracks them up the movie is going to be a smash. But it doesn't work like that. All too often people buy their yachts after the rushes and go bankrupt at the premiere.

Plus, if you don't go to the rushes, you get home earlier. The moment I hear, "Cut!," "Wrap!" I'm off and away.

👓 *No regrets*

I never regret anything. I always said that when I'm old, I want to be sitting there regretting the things I did, not the things I didn't do. And now I'm old, it turns out I don't regret anything at all. Every project I've done has brought me something and has added to the richness of my days. I had fun, and I'm still having it.

There's no point looking back on a flop and thinking, If I knew then what I know now, I wouldn't have done it. I *didn't* know then what I know now. I couldn't have. I made the decision in good faith, for reasons that made sense at the time. And probably I know now what I didn't know then only because I went ahead and did what I wouldn't have done if I'd known it. So I've learnt something.

If I was given the chance to live my life all over again I would do everything the same and remake every single one of my movies, from *Alfie* to *The Swarm*. I had fun, I made wonderful friends, I went to exciting places and I worked with some of the most talented people in the business.

About the only regret I allow myself is that I never got to make *The Dresser* with Orson Welles. In 1963, I was playing the lead in *Next Time I'll Sing to You*, a theatre role that indirectly played a key part in the launch of my film career by bringing me to the attention of Stanley Baker. It also attracted other interest. One night when I was on stage I couldn't help noticing very strong loud laughter coming from the middle of the stalls. I was so struck by it that I tried at one point to look out into the auditorium to see if it was someone I knew. All

I could make out in the gloom was a rather heavy middle-aged man sitting on his own.

After the show I was in my dressing room and there was a knock on my door. I shouted, "Come in," and turned round to find the great filmmaker Orson Welles standing in the doorway. He said some kind things about my performance, which I found somewhat overwhelming, and off he went. We stayed in touch, and many years later Orson approached me about a project he thought we should do together: a film, based on a stage play, about the relationship between a hammy old actor (to be played by Orson) and his devoted gay dresser (me). I knew and loved the play and said yes immediately. I could see that it would be a tremendous vehicle for both of us. Alas, it never happened. Albert Finney and Tom Courtenay had already bought the rights and they made it into a wonderful movie, for which they were both nominated for Academy Awards. Just a few years ago it was remade for the BBC with Anthony Hopkins as the old actor and Ian McKellen as the dresser and it was wonderful all over again. I still sometimes think wistfully of the Orson Welles/Michael Caine version that never got made as the best film I never did.

👓 *Don't let the past control your future*

When you hold a grudge, you're allowing your past—or, worse, what someone else did in the past, for reasons that might have nothing to do with you—to dictate your future. What's the point? What a waste.

Alfred Hitchcock and I became friendly when I was making *Gambit* at Universal Studios in the mid-1960s. Our bungalows were next door to each other (at Universal you didn't have dressing rooms, you had bungalows) and, of course, we were both south Londoners: his family had a shop on the Tower Bridge Road where my maternal grandfather had had a fruit stall. But the friendship didn't last. Alfred offered me the part of a serial killer in a movie called *Frenzy* and I turned it down. It was so brutal and disgusting I just didn't want to do it. Alfred made the movie in 1972 with Barry Foster in the lead role and it did very well but he never spoke to me again.

It wasn't just that we lost touch, as happens with lots of movie friendships. A couple of years later I was filming in Berlin and was walking down the Kurfürstendamm when I saw Hitchcock walking towards me with a group of people. He saw me, he looked at me, and he very deliberately turned his head away and kept walking.

I didn't think about it much at the time, but it came back to me a few years later. As I mentioned before, when we were living in LA in the 1980s one of our favourite restaurants in Beverly Hills was that great Hollywood meeting place Chasen's. A great place to name-drop. One Sunday evening Shakira and I were having dinner there with Frank Sinatra and his wife Barbara, and Gregory Peck and his wife Veronique. I looked across to the table just to the right of the door and there was Alfred Hitchcock. I smiled at him and raised a hand in greeting. He saw me, he looked at me, and he very deliberately turned his head away and kept eating.

I kept glancing at Alfred, sitting on his own, through the rest of the evening. I reflected then that in Hollywood, and elsewhere, if you stop talking to everyone who disappoints you (Vanessa Redgrave and Helen Mirren also turned down parts in *Frenzy*) you're deliberately compounding the disappointment and you certainly don't end up at many dinner parties.

I'm very careful about the grudges I hold. I would never dream of holding a grudge for such a thing. Look at Irwin Allen, who directed me in *The Swarm* and *Beyond the Poseidon Adventure*—talk about disappointments! But I would never let a professional disappointment come in the way of a personal friendship. Irwin became a very dear friend to Shakira and me. He was a generous, warm, fabulous human being, and while we lived in LA we used to eat at Chasen's together most Thursdays.

For me it's about trust. If you break my trust, we can't stay friends, and we can't work together. If I'm going to let something from the past control my future, if I'm going to cut someone out of my life—and I occasionally do—it will be about trust. Because once there's a little weakness in that particular cloth, it may tear at any moment.

👓 Beware of retreading old ground

Remaking movies is a form of looking back that, in general, I would not recommend. Several of my movies have been remade in the last couple of decades, with limited success.

In 2000, my friend Sylvester Stallone remade my 1971 gangster film, *Get Carter*, with Sly himself starring in my original role as Jack Carter and with the action transposed from Newcastle, in the rainy north-east of England, to Seattle, in the rainy northwest of the United States. Sly asked me to come and do a walk-on part for a day as Cliff Brumby—the "big man" played in the original by Bryan Mosley—which I did, thinking it would be fun. It was, but reading the reviews was not.

In 2003, F. Gary Gray did a good job of remaking *The Italian Job* with Mark Wahlberg in the role of Charlie Croker and Charlize Theron (the very beautiful and talented actress who I had worked with on *The Cider House Rules*) stealing the reviews in a new role. And in 2004, Charles Shyer remade *Alfie*, starring Jude Law. Jude is a wonderful actor, whose 2009 *Hamlet* was one of the best I've ever seen (I love *Hamlet*, and have seen a lot, including Richard Burton's in 1964). He did a terrific job with *Alfie* but there were a couple of problems. The 2004 audience was less forgiving than the 1966 audience of Alfie's immature and selfish antics. And at the end of the movie Alfie says, "What's it all about?" My Alfie looks bewildered but Jude's Alfie was more intelligent and self-aware than mine. The moment you see him, you can tell that he knows exactly what it's all about. The movie did not make money and its reviews were mixed.

Despite these red flags, I got involved with the remake of *Sleuth* in 2007, because in my mind this was not really a remake, it was a complete reinvention and, what was more, with a brilliant writer (Harold Pinter), a brilliant director (the wonderful Kenneth Branagh) and a brilliant co-star (Jude Law again). Harold completely rewrote the script, with not a single line of Tony Shaffer's original remaining in his version; and Jude completely reinvented the part I had played in the 1972 original, while I deliberately did not go back and re-watch the movie before taking on the Olivier role. The plot, the characters, the setting and the ending were all changed. We worked our hearts out but the critics were disappointed that it did not improve on the 1972 version and slammed it. We would have been better off moving just a little further away from the original and billing it as an entirely new Pinter piece.

Although it is tempting, for obvious reasons, to remake big hits, I have concluded from painful experience that it's the wrong approach. In remaking good movies you're putting yourself in a no-win situation. The remakes of *Get Carter, Alfie* and *Sleuth* were all disappointments, as was the 2012 remake of *Gambit*, my 1966 movie with Shirley MacLaine, which, despite great writers and a terrific cast, went straight to DVD. They could hardly fail to be: they had a lot to live up to.

In contrast, *Dirty Rotten Scoundrels*, the Frank Oz movie I made with Steve Martin and Glenne Headly in 1988, was a huge hit. It was a remake of the 1964 movie *Bedtime Story*, starring Marlon Brando, David Niven and Shirley Jones, which, despite its excellent cast, had been a flop. It just hadn't been funny. That meant the remake could not be a disappointment: added to which, we reaped the benefits from everything the writers, Stanley Shapiro and Paul Henning, had learnt from what didn't work the first time around. And, by the way, I had an absolute blast making it. Great director, great co-stars, great script, terrific location.

You should really only remake bad movies. It's easy to improve on failure.

👓 When to break the rule and look back

I do make some exceptions. I have allowed myself recently to do a little looking back.

More and more I have been bumping into old friends and reflecting on the journeys we have each taken to bring us to these spots.

When I was young and doing my first TV I played a bit part in a police series called *Dixon of Dock Green* opposite another struggling actor, a wonderful young Canadian called Donald Sutherland. Donald was a terrific and charismatic actor and great fun to be around. A few years later, as my career was just starting to take off, I was cast as Horatio in a BBC TV production of *Hamlet*. The director, Philip Saville, mentioned to me that he had finally, after some difficulty, managed to cast Fortinbras. He explained that though Fortinbras is a small part, who only comes on at the end when everyone else is dead, he has to command the show: in other words, to be a star. "It's very difficult to find an actor with the right star quality who is prepared to play such a small part," he said. I asked who he'd found and he told me, "Donald Sutherland."

Fast forward another ten years and I was making *The Eagle Has Landed* with John Sturges, a great Hollywood director, and a wonderful British cast including Jenny Agutter, Donald Pleasance and Anthony Quayle, plus a great American actor, Robert Duvall. And my co-star was Donald Sutherland who, by then, had starred in *M*A*S*H*; *Klute*, opposite Jane Fonda; and *Don't Look Now*, opposite Julie Christie. We did, I admit, take a moment to look back on where we had come from and to celebrate where we had both come to. (My friendship with Donald was typical of how things work out in the movie business. You get to know people and become very close for a short time, then, because of the way the business works, you don't see each other for years. It is friendship by time and location.) So it was a nostalgic moment when, very recently, I was walking along the street in South Beach, Miami, with my friend and heart doctor, Richard Berger, and I pointed out to Richard the block of flats where I used to live. "Do you know who lives there now?" he said. "Donald Sutherland."

In my latest movie, *King of Thieves*, I appear along

with many old friends: Ray Winstone, Michael Gambon, Jim Broadbent. But maybe the one who gives me the most pleasure is Tom Courtenay. We were young working-class out-of-work actors together in the 1950s and 1960s. Tom broke through with "angry young man" Alan Sillitoe's *The Loneliness of the Long Distance Runner, Billy Liar* and *Doctor Zhivago* just as I was breaking through with *Zulu, Alfie* and *The Ipcress File.* We came together again in *Last Orders* in 2001, and here we were now, with a knighthood each, playing a couple of thieves.

The older I have become, the more moments like this have arisen, and the more I have been tempted by opportunities to look back. And the biggest temptation of all came in the form of *My Generation*, a documentary about Britain in the 1960s and the people who made it. Doing the interviews for the documentary was a great opportunity for me to reconnect with old friends, like Paul McCartney and Twiggy, who I hadn't seen since the 1960s. We had all pursued our fabulous new lives and lost touch, or died. One old friend I regretted not being able to include in the documentary was George Harrison. He lived just down the road from us near Henley at one stage, and we used to go to each other for dinner. One time he brought his guitar and we all sat there eating our dinner in a state of great excitement, thinking he was going to sing for us.

After dinner I said, "I see you brought your guitar, George."

"No, it's not a guitar, Michael."

"Well, what is it, then?" I said, "I saw you bring something in."

"It's a ukulele," he said. "I'm the president of the George Formby Society." And then he gave us a whole concert as George Formby. George Harrison in my dining room doing "Leaning on a Lamp Post" and "When I'm Cleaning Windows."

But, more than that, it was important to me to document this moment in history, when the British working class became their own masters. At the time we didn't have a plan, we weren't organised, we didn't feel part of a movement. We just did what we wanted to do, took no notice of people who said we couldn't, and it turned out, for me and people like me, to be a liberation. It was the best decade ever: it was when everything changed and everything became possible, and I wanted to try to capture all of that, before those who spent the 1960s Looking Back in Anger got too old to remember. This is the kind of looking back that I do allow myself, to make sense of the past and of everything that has happened.

15.

Getting Old and Staying Young

"I've grown old without understanding how I got here."

Youth, 2015

THE OTHER DAY I was minding my own business, having a quiet dinner in a restaurant, when someone approached me with a look I recognised. He had spotted me and wanted a quick word. I looked up from my French onion soup and smiled.

"Are you Michael Caine?"

"Yes, I am," I said.

"Bloody hell," he shot back. "I thought you were a fucking hundred."

That's a back-handed compliment if ever there was one.

I know I'm old but I don't feel old. Not in my head, where it matters. I forget all the time how old I am: it seems like about five years ago I was thirty-five. So I take things on that I shouldn't. I accept scripts. I wheel manure around in the garden. I nearly rupture myself every day. Age, to me, is in the mind. I've seen seventy-year-olds who are already dead, and ninety-year-olds who can't stop themselves living. I stay young by refusing to be old.

The only time I really feel old is when I catch sight of my stand-in on set. A stand-in is someone the same height and build as an actor, whose job is to stand and walk about on set in the actor's place for the hours it takes to get the lighting right. When I first started working, my stand-in was a great-looking young guy and we became good friends. Now I see a poor decrepit old man being helped out of his seat and almost carried to the camera position and with a jolt I realise that's my stand-in. That's me.

Just like I didn't do what I was supposed to in the 1940s and 1950s, when as a working-class lad I was expected to know my place and go and be a fish porter, I don't do what I'm supposed to do now that I'm eighty-five. I'm expected to know my place and sink gracefully back into my sofa. But I don't want to sit down; I don't want to retire; I want to keep on going. And I'm expected to despise old age, and yearn for those golden years of my youth. But I don't do that either and I suspect I'm not alone in that.

Of course ageing brings disappointments and inconveniences, frustrations and indignities, even despair, as weddings and birthday parties give way to hospital visits and memorial services. But it also brings its own joys and even occasionally a little wisdom. I look at ageing not as a problem but as a privilege. As the (old) joke goes—and it isn't really a joke: I can never forget the early deaths of my father, of my childhood friend Paul Challen, who never truly enjoyed good health his entire life and died much too young, of my fellow struggling actors from the early days who gave up on life entirely, of burning talents, like James Dean, Marilyn Monroe, Heath Ledger, who were extinguished too soon—it's better than the alternative.

My approach to old age is, in many ways, like my approach to youth: I still use the difficulty, and I still look for the good in a bad situation, and I still keep striving to do what I love. I enjoy each year so much that as each one slips past I think, I'll have another one of those, please.

👓 *Keep on using the difficulty*

One of the toughest challenges of getting older is that, first, all your idols and mentors get old and die. That's tough. And then, even worse, your friends get old, and some of them go and die as well. But I still maintain there is no difficulty so great it cannot be used. And so, though each blow has been harsh, I have, eventually, been able to use each terrible loss to remind me to enjoy the living, and enjoy my life.

My great hero John Huston died of pneumonia in 1987 at the age of eighty-one. He was funny to the last. At an awards ceremony shortly before he died, he was described as "living legend John Huston." In reply John said, "My doctors assure me that that status will change with the first wintry blast."

I had actually said goodbye to John once already. Several years earlier I had heard the sad news that he was on his deathbed. Sean Connery and I rushed to Cedars-Sinai Hospital in Hollywood to say goodbye, and when we got there he was rambling. "I was in a boxing match," he was saying, "and it turns out the other guy had razors sewn into his gloves and that's why I'm here." John went on about the boxer for twenty minutes, and then Sean and I looked at each other and we were both in tears. We left the hospital, very upset. And then we heard that John had got up and made two more movies. When I saw him I said, "The next time I come to say farewell to you, you'd better bloody die or I'll bloody kill you. Do you know how upset we were?"

John replied, "Well, Michael, you know, people get upset. And people die."

"Yes," I said, "but not twice."

But I was dreadfully upset, of course, the second time John died. He had been an idol of mine, a great supporter of my career, a wonderful director to work with and one of the truly great talents of his era.

I met most of my closest friends in London during the late 1950s and 1960s. Over the years we came to know each other, trust each other, appreciate each other, even love each other. We "Mayfair Orphans," as we named ourselves, all led busy lives but whenever we could we met for lunch or dinner. There were ten of us, but now all but four—the nightclub host Johnny Gold, the composer Leslie Bricusse, the photographer Terry O'Neill and me—are dead.

I miss them terribly. My press agent Theo Cowan was one of the funniest men I've ever come across, with a quiet sadness about him. If you asked him how he was, he'd say, "The hard ones first, eh?" Theo went in the same understated way he had lived his life, settling down for a nap in his office after lunch and never waking up. It was a harsh reminder to us fun-loving Mayfair Orphans that our fun was not going to last for ever.

As one of our group said at his funeral, "They've started bowling in our alley."

But Theo was older than the rest of us and at first the bowling balls came at mercifully long intervals. When I lost my agent Dennis Selinger in 1998 I lost not only an agent but a great guide, counsellor and friend. Dennis had assured us that his cancer was curable but, perhaps for the first time in his life, he was wrong. Or perhaps, I now wonder, he had sensed the truth, but he was being a good agent and true friend to the last: he must have known that the only way I would go to Hollywood to make my movie was if I thought I'd be coming back and seeing him again. There is still a huge Dennis-shaped hole in my life.

Mickie Most, the record producer, was the fittest of us all and we joked that he really must be sick when he cut his daily run down to five miles a day. It was a terrible shock to find out that he actually was—with virulent and incurable lung cancer, caused by the asbestos in the sound studios where he had worked all his life. The last time I saw Mickie, we both knew we would never see each other again but we laughed all the way through lunch. It started when I asked him what the doctor had actually said to him and he said, "I asked him, 'How long have I got?' and he said, 'Put it this way: don't send out any dry cleaning.' " I was still wiping the tears from my eyes as we hugged, then parted outside the restaurant. I turned back for one last look and he had disappeared around the corner of Berkeley Square by the Rolls-Royce showroom. I was crying but, knowing Mickie, he was still probably laughing. That was 2003 and Mickie was just sixty-four.

Five years later we lost Doug Hayward, our tailor and our dear friend, known to us all as the Buddha of Mount Street. It was because Doug would only ever give himself an hour off for lunch that we always used to meet in Mayfair and dubbed ourselves the Mayfair Orphans—although these days it's more often the River Café. But Doug had really left us years before that, his razor-sharp brain ravaged by the cruel indignities of Alzheimer's. When someone has Alzheimer's you know they're going but they take such a long time to go. With Doug, for me, it was like he was walking out of my life over the horizon and taking three years over it. One day I went to see him in his flat above the shop and he was sitting watching television. "Hello, Doug," I said.

He turned, looked at me and said, "Hello." Then he turned back to the television.

That was when I understood that Doug was never coming back.

Someone up there then obviously got his eye in, and we started falling like ninepins. In 2016 we lost trichologist Philip Kingsley, who had always ensured there was not a dandruff-ridden or bald Orphan among us, and less than a year later, Roger Moore. Roger was one of the most genuine, trustworthy and generous people I have ever known. I first met him just after I had made *The Compartment* in 1961, when he was already famous from his TV show *The Saint* and I was very much not.

I was walking along Piccadilly with Terry Stamp and we were thrilled to spot his suave, debonair figure stalking down the street in the opposite direction. He crossed the road towards us, and we looked around us to see if somebody was behind us. But no. He came up to us, smiling, and said, "Are you Michael Caine?" I said I was. "I saw you in *The Compartment*. And I just want to tell you, you're going to be a big star." Roger shook my hand and walked away and I didn't see him again for another five or six years, by which time his prediction had come true. But it was a huge boost for me at the time, and a memorable start to nearly sixty years of friendship.

Then last year, 2017, one bright spring evening, the sun was pouring through the windows when our friend Leslie Bricusse called us from his house in the South of France to tell us that Roger had just died. He had been sick for a while so it was not a surprise but it was still a shock and it still hurt. An hour later, Leslie called again to say that one of my closest Hollywood friends, Jerry Perenchio, the kindest and most charitable rich man I ever met, had just died. I was stunned with sadness. "Leslie, don't take this the wrong way," I said, "I love you, but I really don't want to speak to you again tonight." I went to bed and unplugged the phone.

I have seen people go fast, like Mickie and Theo,

and I have seen people go slow, like Dougie. Both ways have their cruelties, for the individual and for those around them, but I know what I want. I want to live a long life, like Roger, work to the end, like Dennis, laugh my way through lunch, like Mickie, then die in my sleep, like Theo.

It is desperately sad when your family and friends start dying and your close circle gets smaller and smaller. It can be hard to find a way to use the difficulty. And each successive death does not get any easier to bear. I have, though, found that as our little group has become smaller and smaller, it has also become closer and closer. I have also enjoyed getting to know my friends' widows better than I did when their husbands were alive.

Yet another cabbie also made the point to Alec Guinness, in his own inimitable London-cabbie way, that as everyone else your age fades away, there's less and less competition for the good parts. That was many years ago. The great British actors Anthony Quayle, Rex Harrison and Laurence Olivier had all died in quick succession. "Are you an actor?" asked the cabbie.

"I am," said Alec.

"Dropping like flies, aren't you?" I'm sure he didn't mean to sound unkind, and I don't wish to either, but the harsh fact is that the longer you survive as an actor or in any other profession, the lonelier it gets at the top, which is bad for the heart and soul but good for the career.

I feel each loss—my parents and brothers, my idols and mentors, my friends—acutely, and I mourn each one deeply. But for as short a time as possible. I go so deep, I can't stay down there for very long or I would drown. So I come up quickly, gasping for the fresh air of the living. I return with greater interest to those around me who are still here: I see them with fresh eyes and new appreciation.

The other major challenge of getting old is that, even if on the inside you still feel sprightly, on the outside everything starts falling apart. Your looks fade, your eyesight goes, your hearing, your back, your memory. For an actor, this used to mean either retiring gracefully, or ploughing on regardless in a state of denial, chasing after increasingly inappropriate roles.

But, these days, things are different and I have been fortunate that I have been able to use this difficulty too. Just as I was getting old, the baby-boomer audience was getting old with me, and, just as being working-class became fashionable in the 1960s, in the twenty-first century it became fashionable to be old. In 2012, *The Best Exotic Marigold Hotel*, a ten-million-dollar British movie about a bunch of old people living in a hotel in India, took

$150 million at the box office. Producers realised that the generation who had come of age in the 1960s was still very much alive and kicking and wanting to see their lives reflected on the big screen.

Now, instead of turning you out to pasture, they will write parts for you. They will write your lines on the wall or a blackboard if your memory's gone and you can't remember them, and say them in an earpiece if your eyesight's gone as well and you can't read them either. (I haven't had do to that yet, honest, but I've seen it done.)

In fact, not only are there still parts for me: as I have aged, the parts have got more interesting. It's fabulous. Earlier on, it was boy meets girl, boy loses girl, boy regains girl. That was my career. Very glamorous, very show business. But now the old boy—or the old girl—can get anything, lose anything, regain anything. No offence to the girls, but it's much more interesting, much more real.

In the last ten years alone (and I have been "old" for longer than that) I have played, among other things, Alfred the wise father-figure butler in *The Dark Knight* and *The Dark Knight Rises*; Clarence, an ex-magician in the early stages of dementia in *Is Anybody There?*; Harry Brown a lonely ex-Royal Marine turned vigilante on a mission in *Harry Brown*; a very cool spy car, Finn McMissile, in *Cars 2*; NASA physicist Professor Brand in *Interstellar*; symphony orchestra conductor and composer Fred Ballinger in *Youth*; a cartoon gnome (twice) in *Gnomeo and Juliet* and *Sherlock Gnomes* and an elderly bank robber (twice) in *Going in Style* and *The King of Thieves*.

I even managed the unlikely feat, nearly twenty years ago, of being cast as a dead man in *Last Orders*, a tiny, low-budget British picture with the great director Fred Schepisi and a wonderful best-of-British cast, including Helen Mirren, Bob Hoskins, David Hemmings, Tom Courtenay and Ray Winstone, as my son. Although I had only a small part in that movie it was meaningful, not just because of my wonderful fellow actors but because it was the closest I ever came to playing my father.

👓 *Find the good*

One of my all-time favourite movies—in my view terribly underrated—is the 1963 movie *Charade*. It is a romance but also a comedy and a thriller, set in Paris, including a sequence shot in Les Halles, which makes me nostalgic for the times I used to go there for French onion soup at two in the morning, and full of brilliant one-liners from its stars, Cary Grant and Audrey Hepburn. This is one of my favourites:

REGINA (AUDREY HEPBURN): I already know a lot of people and until one of them dies I couldn't possibly meet anyone else.

PETER (CARY GRANT): Well, if anyone goes on the critical list, let me know.

Of course, the line is less funny when you get to my age and the critical list is a mile long. But I have been lucky enough to meet some wonderful new people and make some wonderful new friends in my old age, including the Armenian philanthropists Bob and Tamar Manoukian. Bob and Tamar, now two of our closest friends, are warm and generous people, and exceptional philanthropists. They have taken us to places we had never been, including Armenia and Lebanon, and introduced us to fascinating people from outside our usual world of show business, who we would never normally meet. They also introduced us to the Clooneys at one of their always-memorable dinner parties. I spent a lot of the evening in a slight daze because George and Amal were even more beautiful in real life than they already looked in pictures, and they were also smart, funny, socially engaged and kind. But the point when I knew I had made a new best friend was when George told me about the business he had just sold:

it was a tequila company he had set up with friends to create a tequila you could sip all day and night, straight or on the rocks, without getting a hang-over. We drank a great deal of George's Casamigos tequila that night.

And there has been another miracle to save me from despair and give me new zest for life. The happiest surprise of my long, very happy and very surprising life has been my incredible grandchil-dren: Taylor, who will be ten by the time this book is published, and Allegra and Miles, who will be nine. I consider grandchildren to be God's gift to old people, and I consider being a granddad to be my greatest role to date. They keep me young, and I will do whatever I can to be with them for as many years as I possibly can.

👓 *Keep doing what you love*

Sir John Gielgud, a terrifically gifted actor who died at the age of ninety-six, worked right up until the end of his life. He celebrated his ninetieth birth-day by playing King Lear, with Judi Dench, Eileen Atkins and Emma Thompson as his daughters; he was still ringing his agent at the age of ninety-two to ask him, "Any scripts in this week?"; soon after that he sacked an agent for not getting him a part in the TV adaptation of *David Copperfield*. He also developed a nice line in butlers, winning an Oscar as Dudley Moore's in *Arthur*. I like to keep his example in mind as I continue to refuse to retire.

I have always said anyway that, in the movies, you don't retire, the movies retire you. And they nearly did, in the early 1990s. But since my near-retirement experience, I have enjoyed another whole fulfilling career. My grandson Taylor, who likes to hang out with me in my office, was counting up all my awards the other day, and he pointed out to me that I've won the majority since I hit sixty. When am I going to retire? How about never? Why would I retire when I can keep getting paid doing something I love?

I still love acting so I still do it. But I also love other things—my garden, cooking for family and friends, my grandchildren, time spent with friends, quiet evenings in with Shakira and quiet evenings out with Shakira—so the balance has to be right. My priorities have changed as I've got older. I haven't become one of those old actors you have to watch out for who will make any old piece of rubbish if the money's right. I've been there and done that already so for me now it's the other way around. I've become fussier about what I do.

These days, as well as the obvious things—is the role going to test me, who is the director, what is the script like—I need to know if there's going to be a lot of makeup. Because an early makeup call means getting up in the middle of the night. When he was playing Churchill in *Darkest Hour*, Gary Oldman had to get up at two thirty in the morning to be given his fabulous makeup. I couldn't possibly do that any more. Where is the shoot and what time of year? It has to be somewhere Shakira is prepared to come with me. Not too hot, not too cold, not too damp, not too Spartan. How far is the hotel from the set? If it's an hour's drive, I have to set my alarm clock an hour earlier and I'll arrive back late every evening. What's the budget? If it's too small, that means a budget hotel, a small, cold motor-home on the set and disappointing on-set meals. And, crucially, how much dialogue is there? My memory is still good but I'm past the point where I want to be memorising pages of dialogue, and not yet at the point where I'm prepared to have my lines written down for me on a wall.

In fact, I've become so fussy that I've just done something I've never done before in my life and turned down four movies. One was a fabulous part, but it involved spending two weeks up a Pennsylvanian mountain in the autumn and my first speech was two pages long. When you're old, you feel the cold. One was an excellent script about Alzheimer's that I really wanted to do, but it was so good it upset me just reading it through. With my friend Doug Hayward in mind, I knew I would never get through the scenes without breaking down so, with a heavy heart, I turned it down. And one was a script in which I'm supposed to bathe naked in a Swiss lake in the winter. As I'm coming out of the water, a coachload of tourists come by and stop for their lunch. They see me, and they all stand there laughing and pointing, taking photos of me and my frozen tiny manhood. Seriously. That was a script I was offered. I'm not vain, but I'm also not insane.

These days, if I pick up a script and it says, "Siberia, deepest winter. Our hero trudges through a featureless wasteland...," I put it straight back down again. The only scripts I do are the ones I can't not do: a brilliant script, a director I admire, not too much makeup, not too many lines and an agreeable location. Tick, tick, tick, tick, tick, and I'll be there.

🕶 Don't look back

I don't regret that I'm no longer young. It's a waste of time and, anyway, I've done being young. I had a great time, but now I'm having a great time being old. The 1960s were a crazy buzzing time of excitement and possibility. I loved the stardom that followed, the glitz and glamour of Hollywood. But every decade has been an improvement on the last, and it just keeps getting better. How could I regret being old when the last decade has brought me the joy of my life, my grandchildren? I thought I'd seen it all, done it all, and suddenly I had three grand-children and there was a whole new world of love inside me.

When I go, I know they'll say, "He's had a good old knock. He's had a good innings." I say that my-self when my friends go. But I don't feel like I've had a good innings just yet. I feel like I've just stepped up to the crease. Pass me the bat: there's a few more overs in me yet.

16.

A Life in Balance

"Goodnight, you Princes of Maine, you Kings of New England."

The Cider House Rules,
1999

I HAVE AN EXTRAORDINARY movie family. I have been married to a wonderful array of some of Hollywood's most glamorous and talented women, from Jane Fonda in *Hurry Sundown*, Elizabeth Taylor in *Zee and Company* and Mia Farrow in *Hannah and Her Sisters*, to Glenda Jackson in *The Romantic Englishwoman*, Maggie Smith in *California Suite* and Helen Mirren in *Last Orders*.

My movie children are a quite incredibly talented brood, and I'm very proud of them all, from my first movie child, Demi Moore (I knew there was something good about *Blame It on Rio*), to Ray Winstone in *Last Orders*, Mike Myers in *Austin Powers in Goldmember*, Nicole Kidman in *Bewitched*, Anne Hathaway in *Interstellar* and Rachel Weisz in *Youth*: brilliant, steady and beautiful, inside and out. And although they are not strictly my movie sons I also feel deeply fatherly towards Christian Bale in *Batman Begins, The Dark Knight* and *The Dark Knight Rises*, Tobey Maguire in *The Cider House Rules* and my movie son-in-law in *Inception*, Leonardo Di-

Caprio. Certainly Christian, Tobey and Leonardo are warmly invited to my (imaginary) movie family occasions. I am even blessed with a handful of movie grandchildren.

Extraordinary as my movie family is, my real family is even more so.

My mother and father in their own ways gave me what I needed to go out into the world. I am filled with love and gratitude towards them both. Shakira, Dominique and Natasha helped me to make sense of the world and live well in it. My precious grandchildren, Taylor, Allegra and Miles, were a late-life miracle, who came along when I was seventy-six years old and complete my world.

Shakira, literally and metaphorically, saved my life. I was thirty-eight when I met her, and if it hadn't been for the meaning she provided for me, and the more practical way she pointed out that I was drinking far too much, I would probably have become just one more actor who died an early, promise-unfulfilled, drink-fuelled death. I am still as madly in love with Shakira as when we first met forty-seven years ago. At the risk of repeating myself, she is as beautiful on the inside as she is on the outside—which, as anyone who has met her will attest, is very beautiful indeed—gentle without being weak, funny without a hint of cruelty, poised and confident but not in a way that would ever make anyone else feel inferior. Quite the opposite, she exudes kindness and warmth and has a way of putting everyone around her at their ease.

I'm so proud of both of my smart, kind daughters: Dominique, or Niki as she is to all of us who know and love her, who built herself a fulfilling career and a happy life out of her passion for horses, first as a show-jumper and later as a horse breeder; and Natasha, who has a great business brain and is an interior designer, a nutritionist and a wonderful mother—essentially a single mother—to her three young children.

My grandchildren changed Shakira's and my life completely and brought us a joy I never knew was coming. I take pleasure in every detail of their lives. I live again as I see their faces light up with excitement at pleasures we have come to take for granted, and I have to try hard not to bore my sadly diminishing circle of friends with their exploits. I have lost weight, halved the alcohol and study every health-food article in the newspaper. I obey all my doctors to the letter in an attempt to stay with my precious grandchildren for as long as possible.

My family have given me such confidence, such peace, such joy. And they are a big part of how I have been able to achieve anything I have achieved. They have, almost always, felt complementary to my professional world: a support, not a hindrance or conflict. But, of course, even for someone who has had as much luck as I have there are balances that need to be found.

⌐⌐ *Balance is about choosing*

Even before work/life balance was talked about, it was important to me, although I might not have put it in that way. And for me, balancing my professional and home lives has been mostly about choosing the right projects.

When I was young and struggling I was in no position to choose. I said yes to whatever I was offered and it was still nowhere near enough. It is no coincidence that this was the period of my life when I failed utterly to balance my personal and professional lives. Or, rather, they were in some kind of balance: I failed at both. I would not say that I chose work over family: it was more complicated than that. But at the age of twenty-four my inability to support my wife and beloved baby through the career I longed for filled me with such shame and self-loathing that it led to the breakdown of my first marriage. My wife Pat took Dominique, not yet one, to be brought up by her marvellous and devoted grandparents in Sheffield, and over the next few years I could only rarely afford the train fare to go and see her, let alone the child maintenance I owed her. I ended up divorced, with a daughter I always dearly loved but who, until my career took off, I barely saw and could barely support.

Even as my circumstances were transformed, and I was able at last to be a better father to Dominique, the fear of saying no to offers of work stayed with me. I never really unlearnt the sense of insecurity, the dread of being without work, so I never stopped saying yes. But I did learn to say yes to the right things. And I learnt that the very best thing about stardom and success isn't the money, the fame, the amazing new friends or the best seats in the house, but the freedom to choose.

How did I use that ability to choose? Some would pick out some of my more dubious artistic and commercial choices and say, "Unwisely." But I used it to meet *my* priorities—which changed over time—and to bring the right balance to *my* family's life. I was working hard for success, but at the same time I was making damn sure that success was working hard for me.

In the 1960s, after the success of *Alfie* and *The Ipcress File*, I was acutely conscious of the precariousness of my position. I was a star for the moment, but the choices I made now would determine whether I remained one. I quickly formulated a fairly simple plan. First, I would choose the great roles. Something stretching, something different, something that could show my range. And if none of these came, I would choose the mediocre roles. And if they didn't come either, I would choose the ones that paid the rent. Putting it another way, it was, as they say it should be, always "the script, the script, the script." Apart from when times got hard, when it was "the script, the money, the script, the money." And then, when I got really desperate, "the money, the money, the money." If I wasn't going to win an Academy Award I was at least going to earn my living and keep working. Unlike major stars, such as, say, Clint Eastwood, Robert Redford or Paul Newman, I had no concerns about letting down my fans by taking this role or that: I was an actor and I needed to work.

In 1971, Shakira walked into my life and turned it upside down in the best way possible, and not long afterwards our darling baby Natasha arrived and, though I hadn't thought it possible, made my life even more perfect. My priorities changed and my decision-making changed with them. It was still about the stretching roles, and keeping working, but now there was another layer. Now I looked for roles that would allow me to stay with my wife and baby, either filming near our home in England or somewhere agreeable where a mother and young child could happily join me. Shooting in rural Tanzania and squatting in huts in the local village? Or—and I did actually do this, on *Too Late the Hero*, pre-Shakira—shooting in a humid, insect-infested Philippines jungle and living for twenty-two weeks in a half-built massage parlour? The rooms were only ever expected to be used for brief encounters and every expense had been spared in furnishing and decorating them. (And we could really have shot it in the tropical garden at Kew. It was just us looking at a load of palm trees.) No, thank you. Shooting in Paris and staying in the George V? No problem. You have probably never heard of *The Marseille Contract*, released in the United States as *The Destructors* in 1974. And you don't need to: despite the presence of Anthony Quinn and James Mason, it was a flop. But I didn't care. It got Shakira and new-born baby Natasha, who had both been through the wringer, out of that bitter English winter and into the comparative warmth of the South of France.

By the 1980s I was experienced enough that I was layering in some other important factors. It was still about a challenging role and a pleasant location, but it was also about a great script (you can win an Academy Award for some of the easiest acting of your career with a brilliant script) and a director I admired and wanted to work with. In any walk of life, it's never just about your own job description. It's about the boss, your colleagues, the quality of the work and how it fits with your personal life.

That was how I came to turn down a film co-starring Sally Field, who had just won an Oscar for *Norma Rae*, and instead accept the role of Frank in *Educating Rita* opposite Julie Walters, who had played a blinder as Rita on stage but had never appeared in a film. The role was a wonderful stretch for me; the director was Lewis Gilbert, who had directed me in *Alfie*; and the wonderful screenplay was by Willy Russell, who had adapted it from his own novel and play. As a bonus, it was funny—comedy is so hard to write that a good one is like gold dust. And as the cherry on top, the story was one I felt honoured to tell, about working-class lives and the power of education.

And, of course, that was also how I was able to give an immediate yes to Chris Nolan, when he turned up that Sunday morning, script in hand, wanting to know whether I would like to play Alfred Pennyworth, Batman's butler. Was it a great role? Yes. He's the toughest butler you ever saw: he serves drinks but he's also a trained killer. Was there a great script? Yes again. A great director? Absolutely. An agreeable location? Could hardly have been better: we'd be shooting at Shepperton, the studios where I'd appeared in my first movie, *A Hill in Korea*, in 1956. It was extraordinary to walk in there and appear again on the sound stage where I had spoken (or, rather, forgotten) my first ever lines in a movie. And for bonus points: a terrific cast of brilliant old friends and exciting new talent.

As my family grew up, my priorities continued to shift. When my mother needed a new house, I did *Jaws: The Revenge*. My agent Dennis Selinger thought it was a poor decision but my bank manager loved it (and Mum did too). When my daughter Natasha became old enough to watch movies I realised that it would be years until she would be able to watch any of mine, which were all unsuitable viewing for a child. That was how I came to play Scrooge in *The Muppet Christmas Carol*, a great experience at the time because the puppeteers are such gentle folk, and a recurring joy every Christmas when we watch it all together as a family.

Thirty years and another generation later, I started getting the urge to make another children's movie. I couldn't let my grandchildren watch *Harry Brown* any more than Natasha could have watched *Get Carter*, but since they had been born in a period of just over eleven months I had become quite a cartoon connoisseur: the biggest TV in the house was in my office and the children wouldn't watch TV anywhere else. In fact Taylor, aged two, decided that my office was his office. If you called, "Taylor, where are you?" he would shout back, "I'm in my office!"

and if you asked him to come and he didn't want to, he would say, "I'm working!" So, when I was approached to voice Finn McMissile in *Cars 2*—a 1966 pale blue Aston Martin, about the coolest car I'd ever heard of—I jumped at the chance. Cartoons, or animated features as I believe they're known now, have come on a long way since Mickey Mouse and Donald Duck. *Cars 2*, which, apart from anything else, was the first 3D movie I had ever seen or been involved in, was absolutely astonishing to me.

I also made *Journey 2: The Mysterious Island*, based on the Jules Verne story and shooting in the Hawaiian jungle, which, I'm pleased to report, was situated close to an enormous shopping mall and seemed to contain no insects—or, anyway, none that wanted to bite me. And I voiced Lord Redbridge in *Gnomeo and Juliet* and *Sherlock Gnomes*. One movie for each grandchild and one for luck. Although things don't stand still, do they? Grandchildren in particular. The other day they wanted to watch a movie so I started scrolling through the kids' movies section on Sky. "What are you doing?" my still-nine-year-old grandson Taylor protested. "We're not kids any more."

"Yeah," said eight-year-old Allegra.

"Yeah," said her twin brother, Miles.

"What do you want to see, then?" I asked them.

"Vin Diesel," shouted Taylor, and his younger siblings did not demur.

Slightly saddened at this loss of innocence, I quickly rallied and found them a movie called *The Last Witch Hunter*, featuring Vin Diesel, Elijah Wood, Rose Leslie and Granddad. Honour was satisfied all around.

I have often been tempted to choose a picture for the pleasure of working with old friends. With mixed results. Working in Chris Nolan's repertory company has been nothing but a pleasure and brought me nothing but commercial and artistic success. On the other hand *Bullseye*, which I made with Michael Winner and Roger Moore, could not have been more inappropriately named. We had a blast making it but, as far as I could tell, no one got any pleasure from watching it and it never came close to hitting any target. The 1998 movie *Curtain Call*, co-starring Maggie Smith, with whom I had had success with *California Suite*, and directed by my old friend Peter Yates, went straight to DVD. Working with friends, I have concluded, is an added bonus when everything else—role, script, director—is right. When any of those things is wrong, having friends around will make things more fun, but it won't fix the movie.

ᴖᴖ *Balance is about boundaries*

I have balanced my work and family partly by bringing them together and partly by keeping them strictly apart.

In keeping the two halves of my life apart, I was lucky that I was always able to compartmentalise. I never brought my work stress home ("Don't watch the rushes") and I never took my home stress to work ("Relax, focus, be in the moment"). When I'm in the studio, nothing exists but the studio, and when I'm at home, nothing exists but home.

In bringing my two lives together, I have been extremely fortunate in my choice of wife. Shakira is no little woman married to the big film star: we are equal partners in our marriage and in our professional life and Shakira's off-screen contribution to our success is as important as what I do in front of the cameras. But, while Shakira is no one's appendage, she has been prepared to come with me as a partner everywhere I go. I haven't gone off on location and made a load of new friends she doesn't know—or, even worse, created a real-life alternative movie family. She hasn't stayed at home and created a home life that has no space for me when I come back. Parallel lines, as they taught me in geometry, never meet. So we have kept our lines and our lives well and truly intertwined.

We tried being apart only rarely and it never worked. In the early days of our courtship we were apart for a few days and missed each other terribly. Twenty years later I was so desperate for work that I accepted a role in *On Deadly Ground*, breaking several of my rules (if you're going to do a bad movie, at least do it in a good location; if Shakira won't go, don't go). Shooting in Alaska, the work froze my brain and the weather froze my arse. I vowed never again.

The very happiest times of my life have been when I've been able to get my work and my family into the most complete and satisfying balance. Until very recently, I always said that the happiest movie I ever made—the one I had the most fun making—was *Dirty Rotten Scoundrels*. The director was Frank Oz, a kind and gentle man and fantastic comedy director, nothing like his alter ego, Miss Piggy, in *The Muppets*. He was much more like Grover from *Sesame Street*, or Yoda from the *Star Wars* movies, whom he also voices.

I had worked with Frank on *The Muppet Christmas Carol* and had great trust in him. My co-stars were Steve Martin, who I knew, admired and liked a lot—he is actually quite a shy, reserved person when he's not putting on a zany on-screen persona, and though he is best-known for his comic acting he is also an incredibly talented writer and musician—

and Glenne Headly, who I had never heard of at the time but turned out to be fabulous as a performer and a person.

On set, we barely stopped laughing. The script was genuinely funny—I still think this is the funniest movie I ever made—while avoiding ever being cruel. And, best of all, this was not going to be one of those movies set on the French Riviera but shot in some decaying Eastern European resort (this was before the Berlin Wall came down and Eastern European resorts spruced themselves up). "It's set in summer in the South of France," said Frank, "so we shoot in summer in the South of France." A man after my own heart. The French Riviera is a magical place, full of incredible beaches, unforgettable restaurants and beautiful people—present company excluded.

We rented a villa close to our friends Roger and Luisa Moore and Leslie and Evie Bricusse, and as it was the school holidays a teenage Natasha and two of her friends were able to join us, even working as extras for a couple of days and earning themselves some pocket money. Paradise in paradise.

I didn't think anything would ever top that but recently I had an even more joyful experience, making *Going in Style*, a comedy heist movie about three old men who lose their pensions and get so desperate that they decide to rob a bank. Like *Dirty Rotten*

Scoundrels and *Educating Rita*, the script was that rare thing, a truly funny comedy. My co-stars were Morgan Freeman, with whom I had made at least half a dozen movies, and Alan Arkin, who, though I had never worked with him before, was a joy to work with and soon felt like an old friend. The director, Zach Braff, was young and brilliant. And the movie was a story I felt excited to tell. Although it was a comedy it was also making some serious points about the struggles of the working class in the United States: three old men lose their pensions, with devastating consequences: they forfeit their homes and cannot access health care. Eventually they hatch a plan to rob the bank that is to blame for the collapse of their lives.

But what really set this movie apart was its location. If you were to ask me today for my perfect job, I would say, "A great script, a great director, great co-stars, shooting somewhere pleasant and warm near the sea, in my grandchildren's school holidays." And that was what *Going in Style*, miraculously, turned out to be. Just as I loved taking Shakira with me, and Natasha when she wasn't at school, now I love going everywhere I can with my grandchildren. The movie was shot in New York, a city I know and love and, more importantly, where Shakira's family lives. I found a house on the beach in Sands Point, thirty minutes from the shoot, and installed the entire family there

for seven weeks. Shakira's mother, Saab, had been un-
well and had not seen her great-grandchildren for two
years. I found her a chair and a cup of tea, and placed
her in a spot where she could sit and watch them,
whatever they were doing, scampering in and out of
the pool and the sea, all day. And every so often one of
them would run up and give her a kiss and a cuddle
and pad off again. Heaven for her. And coming home
to that house after a day's shooting was heaven for me.
Going in Style was the happiest film I ever made.

I regard the family as the greatest organisation ever
created by human beings. And, in spite of all the
wonderful things that Fate has given me, I regard
my own happy family—Shakira, my daughters Dominique and Natasha and my grandchildren Taylor,
Allegra and Miles—as my greatest achievement and
the best thing that has ever happened to me. Probably as a reaction to the Christmases of my childhood
when we received plenty of love but not much else,
Christmas is an extravaganza, with presents galore,
decorations everywhere, the biggest tree the room
will hold, loads of crackers, a huge turkey and a
crowd of family and friends. Family celebrations—
and we celebrate everything we can think of—are
happy, noisy affairs, with small presents, lots of easy
food, gallons of ice cream and always, between the
main course and dessert, a song-and-dance show from

the children. They go off and rehearse while the adults are eating their dinner, then come back with wonderful entertainments for us. Taylor directs, and there is always a musical interlude, with Miles singing, or an improvised dance, to give Allegra time to execute an elaborate costume change for the finale.

I adore the shows for themselves but also because they're such a clear marker of how the children are growing up and how their personalities are advancing: when they were four and five years old, we in the audience didn't know what they were doing, but neither did they. And now they're eight and nine, they're so sharp and talented and clever, each trying to outperform the others. Holidays together are sheer bliss. Our latest was in Barbados, my favourite holiday destination in the world, where we stayed as guests of my friend Andrew Lloyd Webber—a musical genius and a great host—and his brilliant wife Madeleine. It is a beautiful place, up the hill from the beach for a bit of privacy, and I sat in paradise, writing this book and watching my grandchildren running in and out of the sea where their mother learnt to swim. I also got caught by a member of the paparazzi walking on my crutch (remember the broken ankle) past a poster that said, "Astonishingly enough, I don't give a shit." But, quite honestly, I was so happy, I didn't.

But it doesn't need to be a holiday or a celebration.

I'm overwhelmed every day with gratitude at the happiness my family brings me. They are my legacy, my contribution to society, my joy. I have had a wonderful career and enjoyed it all, but I can honestly say that they mean more to me than all the movies and awards put together. No Hollywood moment can beat the moments I first set eyes on each of my children and grandchildren. Glitz, glamour and stardust are all very well but they cannot give you a warm, sticky-fingered hug on a rainy night. So, if you'll excuse me, I'm heading off now to kick a football around the garden with the grandchildren.

Epilogue

I HAVE GONE FROM my first role as a butler with one line in a draughty theatre in Horsham—"Dinner is served"—to Batman's butler in three blockbuster movies; from playing the poker-faced spy in *The Ipcress File* to self-satire in *Austin Powers in Goldmember*; from my early years in rep to winding up back there again, as part of Christopher Nolan's great movie-making repertory family; from an unknown Harold Pinter's first play, *The Room*, at the Royal Court in 1960, to his last work, the re-made *Sleuth*; from Alfie to Alfred, and from Harry Palmer to Harry Brown—an old man who started out, like me, in the Elephant and Castle but who, unlike me, never left. As I sit here in my riverside apartment, looking out over the Thames at London being rebuilt all around me, and remember, as a child, sitting in a bomb shelter and listening to it being destroyed, I can't help reflecting that life has a way of coming full circle.

But it has also, luckily, moved on. I have just spent a happy morning watching the wedding of two people very much in love: Prince Harry and Meghan Markle, a divorced, mixed-race, independent-minded, feminist American woman. What would once have been unthinkable is now embraced and celebrated. Things have changed for the better in terms of class, too. Looking back, I like to think I played a small part in the social revolution of the 1960s, that I helped working-class people to say, "I can do anything." My father left school at fourteen, I went to grammar school until I was sixteen and my daughter Natasha went to university: her graduation was one of the proudest days of my life, but for her children, my grandchildren, it will be just a normal thing.

Looking forward, I am a feminist, an anti-racist and an optimist. And my hope is that, just as brilliant writers wrote the parts that made me, new generations of brilliant writers will write the parts for all those who have not yet been given their turn. John Osborne urged us to Look Back in Anger but I prefer to Look Back in Joy and to Look Forward in Hope. If you are young and just starting out, don't hesitate, don't be afraid. Jump right in. Go for it. A better time is coming, and you can be part of it.

I have been enormously lucky. My seemingly impossible dreams really have come true. I have done everything I wanted to do, been everywhere I wanted to go and met everyone I have ever wanted to meet. But if I hadn't been lucky, I would have kept going anyway, doing something I loved and trying to do it as well as I possibly could. In the end if I could give you one bit of advice, it would be that: find what you love, and do it as well as you can. Pursue your dream and, even if you never catch it, you'll enjoy the chase. The rest comes down to luck, timing and God: even if you don't believe in him, he believes in you. And when all of that runs out, use the difficulty.

If you've got this far, I thank you for joining me on the trip: through the happy times and the misery, the rough and the smooth, the low moments and the amazing highs. I hope you've learnt something that helps you, too, along the way. For myself, I've had such a great time following my dreams that when my time comes I'd like to come back as me and do it all over again.

John Wayne gave me one last piece of advice and I want to pass it on to you now. It was 1979 and he was fighting cancer in the UCLA Medical Center, in a room two doors down from Shakira, who was recovering from life-threatening peritonitis. Every day when I went in to visit Shakira, I would pop in to see the Duke. I don't remember what we talked about—old friends and old times, I suppose. I do remember how brave he was as he faced up to his impending death. "It's got me this time, Mike," he said to me, with a smile, as though it was a fair fight but the Big C had drawn first. "I won't be getting out of here." And then, seeing I was close to tears, "Get the hell out of here and go and have a good time."

The Duke got it right that time. So go on. Get the hell out of here and go and have a good time. What the hell—go and blow the bloody doors off!

Acknowledgments

THE IDEA FOR THIS book came in part from a master class on movie acting that I recorded for the BBC many years ago, and the book *Acting in Film* that was based on it. Coming across it again recently, I realised that, while a lot of what I was on about was quite technical, there were lessons in there that could work for everyone. And in the almost thirty years since I recorded that master class—has it really been that long?—this old dog had learnt a few new tricks to pass along too. So my first acknowledgement is to myself thirty years ago for making the master class, and to Maria Aitken, Nathan Silver and everyone else involved in its production.

No endeavour ever succeeds without a tremendous team effort from people who are all expert at what they do, and this book is no exception. I would like to thank Caroline Michel, who got things started, and my skilled and supportive editors, Rowena Webb in London and Paul Whitlatch in New York, who took it from there. My thanks to all of those in the team at Hodder, especially Karen Geary, Juliet Brightmore, Lucy Hale, Catriona Horne and Alasdair Oliver. And thank you to Deborah Crewe: without her help I couldn't have written the bloody book.

Thank you to Toni Howard, for watching my back, and to legal genius Barry Tyerman, my agent in England Kate Buckley-Sharma, my PA Teresa Selwyn and John Davis.

My biggest debt in this and so many other endeavours is to my wife Shakira, who is my rock, and so much more. Thank you to Shakira, to my wonderful friends and family, and to my grandchildren Taylor, Miles and Allegra, the next generation, who are in my mind and my heart every day.

Image Credits

p. xiv: London, 1965. Photo by Philippe Le Tellier/ Paris Match via Getty Images

p. 3: With mother at home, 1964. Photo © Mirrorpix

p. 29: Dressing room, 1965. Photo by Larry Ellis/Express/Getty Images

p. 53: *The Ipcress File,* 1965. Photo by Universal Studios/Getty Images

p. 71: *The Compartment,* 1965. BBC / Ronald Grant Archive / Mary Evans

p. 94: At home, c.1995. Photo © Terry O'Neill/Iconic Images

p. 97: *Sleuth,* 1973 with Laurence Olivier. Entertainment Pictures / Alamy Stock Photo

p. 111: *Zulu,* tea break, 1963. Photo by Silver Screen Collection/Hulton Archive/Getty Image

p. 133: *The Quiet American,* 2002. AF archive / Alamy Stock Photo

p. 151: *Educating Rita,* 1983 with Julie Walters. Photo by Manchester Daily Express/SSPL/Getty Images

p. 169: *Alfie,* 1966 with Lewis Gilbert. Everett Collection Inc / Alamy Stock Photo

p. 191: On set of *Dressed to Kill,* 1980. Photo by Hulton Archive/Getty Images

p. 208: Cannes, 2015. Photo by Nicolas Guerin/Contour by Getty Images

p. 211: Oscar for Best Supporting Actor, *The Cider Houes Rules,* Academy Awards 2000. REUTERS/Mike Blake

p. 239: *Batman Begins,* 2005. AF archive / Alamy Stock Photo

p. 265: *Alfie,* 1966 with Jane Asher. Photo by Silver Screen Collection/Getty Images

p. 287: *Dirty Rotten Scoundrels,* 1988 with Steve Martin. Photo © Terry O'Neill/Iconic Images

p. 305: *Youth,* 2015, photo call in Cannes with Rachel Weisz. Splash News / Alamy Stock Photo

p. 325: With Natasha, Shakira and Niki. REUTERS/Fred Prouser

p. 344: With grandchildren, 2018. Photo © Andrew Fairbrother

p. 348: *The Italian Job,* 1969 with Michael Standing. Photo by Paramount/Getty Images